Incredible Plant-Based Desserts

INCREDIBLE

Plant-Based

DESSERTS

Colorful
Vegan Cakes,
Cookies, Tarts, and
other Epic Delights

ANTHEA CHENG

Brimming with creative inspiration, how-to projects, and useful information to enrich your everyday life, Quarto Knows is a favorite destination for those pursuing their interests and passions. Visit our site and dig deeper with our books into your area of interest: Quarto Creates, Quarto Cooks, Quarto Homes, Quarto Lives, Quarto Drives, Quarto Explores, Quarto Gifts, or Quarto Kids.

First Published in 2019 by Quarry Books, an imprint of The Quarto Group,
100 Cummings Center, Suite 265-D, Beverly, MA 01915, USA.
T (978) 282-9590 F (978) 283-2742 QuartoKnows.com

Quarry Books titles are also available at discount for retail, wholesale, promotional, and bulk purchase. For details, contact the Special Sales Manager by email at specialsales@quarto.com or by mail at The Quarto Group, Attn: Special Sales Manager, 100 Cummings Center, Suite 265-D, Beverly, MA 01915, USA.

10 9 8 7 6 5 4

ISBN: 978-1-63159-718-3

Digital edition published in 2019
eISBN: 978-1-63159-719-0

Library of Congress Cataloging-in-Publication Data is available.

Design and page layout: Timothy Samara
Photography: Anthea Cheng

Printed in China

Please see your health-care provider before beginning any new health program

*This book is dedicated to my social media
and blog audience. To every customer
who has purchased a treat or cake from
me. To every person who has attended my
workshops and pop-up events. Without you,
this book wouldn't exist and I wouldn't be able
to fill my life with creative projects!*

———

*I would also like to dedicate this
to my partner, Dan, who has supported me
through thick and thin and made me
laugh at every hour.*

———

*Also, to my late best friend, Michelle, who
consistently supported everything I did.
Your passing has taught me to appreciate the
people and things in my life while I can.*

Contents

My Story

AN INTRODUCTION

Hello! My name is Anthea and welcome! I have a blog and social media account called *Rainbow Nourishments* and used to have a cake business. In my daily life and in this book, I share colorful vegan treats and a flexible approach to wholesome eating. Many of the recipes in this book have options with refined sugar and without, with gluten and without . . . you can pretty much "pick your own adventure!" And although most cake business owners keep their recipes a trade secret, I'll be sharing many of my secret recipes in this book.

But this isn't just a cookbook with dessert recipes. It's about connecting with loved ones and positive memories. It's about being kind to yourself, those around you, and the environment. One of my first memories with food is from when I was about five years old. My brothers and I ran around hot plates, waitstaff, and customers at my parents' restaurant. We hid our soft toys in a laundry chute and found them "magically" transported to the basement with dirty tea towels and chef clothes. I'd arrange my toys as if they were sitting in a classroom, ask what they wanted for lunch, and serve them while happily humming away. You know when you visit a restaurant or small business and you see a kid in the corner playing or bored out of their mind? Yep, that was us.

My parents migrated from Hong Kong (China) to Sydney, Australia, in the 1970s. Although my father previously worked in a bank and my mother aspired to be an accountant or a nurse, this was impossible in a country where they weren't confident with the primary language, English. Like many other Chinese migrants, they worked in hospitality to make ends meet. My father is the kind of person who likes to do *everything* so their restaurants provided many types of food. Their repertoire included classic Australian fish and chips, Chinese, Italian, French, Thai, Singaporean, and the list goes on.

We often talked about the family business at the dinner table, and the little time outside school hours, tutoring, and extracurricular activities was spent at the restaurant. People often romanticize about wanting to own a cafe or restaurant, but our lives were anything but glamorous! My work clothes always smelled like the deep fryer and customers' cigarette smoke. My mother's knees were constantly in pain, and we barely saw our father outside the restaurant.

I was determined (or desperate) to have a career outside of food, so I studied and worked as much as humanly possible. Fortunately, I graduated with honors at university, and I had a strong career in political and humanitarian issues. I left all my friends and family to work interstate for a large federal government department.

After several years, I became extremely mentally and physically ill. I knew a lot of this was due to living in a new city away from loved ones. I needed to recover, so in 2015, I created a hobby Instagram account to connect with like-minded individuals. *Rainbow Nourishments* was a way for me to share the weird and wacky things I was making at home and the "rainbow" of ways I was nourishing myself. After a few twists and turns, I quit my secure government job to work on *Rainbow Nourishments* full-time.

Learning from the struggles of my parents and my childhood, I wanted to make *Rainbow Nourishments* less about the kitchen and more about connecting with people on a deeper level. It grew into a large social media account and blog that shared wholesome vegan recipes and promoted discussion about wellbeing and the environment. It became a cake business, providing treats to the most popular cafes in my city, for weddings, birthdays, and special events. I now develop recipes with large and small corporations, and I act as a food consultant to dessert businesses around the world. I host many pop-up events, including high teas, dinners, and workshops, in Australia and internationally. The recipes in this book come from my professional experience and also a place of love and kindness.

WHY VEGAN?

To be honest, it actually took me ten years to fully transition to a vegan lifestyle! However, it is a reminder to always listen to your body and to take things at your own pace.

When I was fourteen, I stopped consuming meat or anything with eggs and dairy in it. I disliked the taste, and I became aware of the impact it was having on my health and the

environment. I knew that consuming fewer animal products would significantly decrease my high cholesterol, which I was genetically predisposed to.

However, at that age, I was living at home in a meat-orientated environment, and I was unable to maintain a balanced vegan diet with adequate food and nutrition. I wasn't eating enough and was malnourished, so my body started shutting down. Unfortunately, due to this, I went back to my prevegan ways but avoided consuming dairy. But I knew that, one day, I would try to go vegan again.

Around ten years later, I was living out of the family home and I tried to have a lifestyle that had a minimal impact on the environment. I recycled everything I could, walked almost everywhere, bought secondhand clothes, used no plastic bags, and the list goes on. Facts were emerging such as it takes six times more water to produce beef than pulses per gram of protein, as identified by UNESCO's Institute for Water Education. I realized that there was no such thing as humanely killing an animal that wants to live.

I asked myself: If I'm so conscious about the environment, why am I still *choosing* to consume meat and animal products? Why am I *choosing* to do all those things to the environment?

I was still consuming animal products out of "convenience" because I didn't want to inconvenience non-vegan family and friends. I re-evaluated my values and started acting on them, so I became vegetarian, then vegan. For once, I was doing something that I actually believed in. And, unlike when I was in my teens, I was able to create dishes that were nutritionally balanced.

During the last five years, minimalism or the idea of consuming less has grown significantly. Plant-based diets fit perfectly in this movement as eating no animal products significantly reduces a person's carbon footprint. In addition, eating wholefoods instead of convenience foods will help minimize plastic and unnecessary packaging.

I realize that it isn't possible for everyone to adopt a plant-based diet or eat unpackaged wholefoods all the time. I think it is important to have a healthy relationship with food, listen to your own body, and have the lifestyle that is right for you. Despite this, I still think most people would benefit from a diet with more vegetables, fruit, and wholefoods. After all, it is about making changes that are sustainable and can be maintained in the long-term.

LIVING WITH KINDNESS

Rainbow Nourishments isn't just about colorful vegan food. It's about the "rainbow" or diversity of ways that people can nourish themselves.

I follow a plant-based, wholefoods diet, but my ultimate goal is to have a healthy relationship with food, so I don't seek "perfection" with eating wholefoods. In that light, this book contains some refined sugar and gluten. Sometimes, treats simply taste better with these ingredients! It is so important to have a wholesome life where you spend time away from preparing and thinking about food. If you've had a busy day and feel exhausted, it's okay to get some take-out with refined oils and processed carbohydrates rather than pushing yourself to create something in the kitchen. After all, I do love crunchy fries and pizza! It's important to listen to those cravings.

Many people criticize themselves when they fall short of their expectations with a diet, lifestyle, or activity. Like many, I'm constantly on a journey to practice better self-talk and self-compassion. If I notice I'm being overly critical of myself, it helps to remind myself that I did or am doing the best I can with what I have, know, and feel. It can be easy to be your own worst enemy but, if you can, it helps to talk to yourself like a good friend would talk to you.

As much as I love preparing and creating dishes, I don't want my life to be surrounded by food. Some self-care activities that I love doing outside the kitchen include:

Spending time with close family and friends soaking up some sun

Going on gentle walks or hikes in nature

Gardening . . . and occasionally researching why my pot plants are dying (ha-ha)

Drawing and doodling whatever comes to mind

Coloring in adult coloring books

Reading whatever I feel like

Watching television, movies, or videos that genuinely make me happy and where I'm not tempted to compare myself to others

Most of these activities tread gently on the Earth and align with my personal values. It's important to find activities that suit you and your lifestyle! I strongly believe that incorporating self-care activities in your everyday life helps you maintain positive mental health and, in turn, helps you to have a healthy relationship with food.

Things you will need

Equipment That Will Make Your Life Easier

There are a few items in my kitchen that I use almost every day, and they will be needed for some of the recipes in this book. Having efficient equipment makes cooking so much more enjoyable! After all, life is meant to be enjoyed, right?!

HIGH-POWERED BLENDER

If I could only have one kitchen appliance, it would definitely be my high-powered blender! Blenders are best for liquids, such as smoothies and the creamy part of cheesecakes. With a high-powered blender, I can turn whole cashews into a smooth cream that will just melt in my mouth. A conventional blender will not do this or will take much longer to do this . . . and after some time, your blender will probably die. (I speak from experience.) A high-powered blender may be an investment, but it is one to make if you love making vegan desserts!

FOOD PROCESSOR

A food processor is great for chopping and processing coarse ingredients, such as nuts and dates for cake bases. If you have a food processor with multiple attachments, you can use it to grate vegetables for salads . . . or carrots for cake, of course! Alternatively, you can chop the ingredients by hand, but this will take much more time and patience.

STAND MIXER

Although not necessary, a stand mixer will help a lot! It's great for mixing large amounts of cake batter, for whipping coconut cream, and for making meringues! It will mix and whip batters that other machines cannot do efficiently. An alternative is to use an electric hand mixer or a hand whisk, which work well for shorter mixing tasks.

STICK BLENDER

I love using my stick blender when I need to blend or emulsify a small amount of liquid and don't want to use my bigger blender. This includes chocolate and berries for making chia jam! I'd prefer to use a stick blender for 5 seconds rather than mixing something for 5 to 10 minutes. Plus, there is minimal washing up!

CAKE MOLDS AND PANS

For bars, large tarts, and cakes, I prefer using loose-bottom or springform pans because treats can easily be removed from them. For small cheesecakes and tarts, I love using silicon molds as I don't need to line them with parchment paper and the treats will usually pop out easily! If you don't have one of those pans, line your pan with parchment paper along the bottom and sides and remove your treat by pulling up the sides of the parchment paper or turning your pan upside down onto a plate.

MAKING DESSERTS WITH VEGAN, GLUTEN-FREE, AND REFINED SUGAR-FREE INGREDIENTS

—

I strongly believe that "free-from" desserts and meals should taste as delicious as—or even better than—their conventional versions. Everybody should have access to delicious food! After decades of making treats for family, friends, and customers, I have found ways to make cakes fluffy, cheesecakes creamy, and to create everything else that I love about desserts. I have tested many substitutions and included only my favorites in this book for the sake of simplicity and reducing waste.

DAIRY ALTERNATIVES

In many countries, it is becoming easier to find plant-based substitutes for many dairy products.

Soy, almond, coconut, and oat milk. Any of these plant-based milks can easily replace dairy milk. In baked treats, you can substitute milk with water, although this will create a treat that is less moist and flavorsome.

Coconut cream. I love using coconut cream as it is accessible and affordable. For cheesecakes and whipped cream, I use canned coconut cream, which has no emulsifiers, and I use only the thickest part of the cream that has risen to the top of the can. The liquid at the bottom of the can be reserved for smoothies and soups. I use a brand of coconut cream that has around 35% fat where most of the can is filled with beautiful, thick cream.

For unbaked cheesecakes, if you're unable to source a coconut cream with a high amount of fat, use the highest fat coconut cream you can find and add a little more coconut oil or cacao butter to compensate for it. If you don't do this, your cake will not set or it will be a little softer.

Plant-based oils, such as sunflower and olive. Butter adds moisture to conventionally baked treats, but it can be replaced with light-tasting vegetable oils, vegan butter, and sometimes nuts. My preference is sunflower oil as many of my treats already include whole sunflower seeds, and it has a minimal taste and is affordable. If you don't mind the taste of olive oil in your baked treats, you can use that instead.

EGG SUBSTITUTES

Eggs are often used to bind and leaven ingredients in conventional baked desserts. As eggs have multiple purposes, there is no single substitute for eggs in vegan baked desserts. Not all recipes need egg substitutes, so I have only included them where necessary. For each recipe, I have tested various egg substitutes and included the one that provided the best result. Here are some of my favorites:

Ground chia seeds or flaxseeds can be combined with water to form a chia/flax egg that helps bind the ingredients in some pastries, cookies, and cakes. An egg can be replaced by 1 tablespoon (13 g) of chia or (12 g) flaxseeds (ground up) mixed with 3 tablespoons (45 ml) of water. For simplicity, I have incorporated these quantities into some recipes so you don't have to make a chia/flax egg in addition to the other steps.

Baking powder helps baked desserts set and rise. For some cakes, I added baking powder in addition to self-rising flour to give an extra lift.

Aquafaba is the liquid leftover from canned chickpeas or other pulses, or from cooking dried chickpeas or pulses. It is relatively new in the vegan baking world, and it can be used to bind ingredients in baked treats. It can also be whipped like egg whites to make meringues and marshmallows!

Whenever I open a can of chickpeas, I put the aquafaba in an ice tray or container. Then, I freeze it, so I have it on hand whenever I'm baking.

GLUTEN-FREE ALTERNATIVES

I do not follow a gluten-free diet, but many of my cake business customers have requested quality gluten-free cakes! Baking without gluten and animal products is notoriously difficult, but I endeavored to develop accessible and tasty recipes. Many supermarkets, health food shops, or South Asian/Indian shops sell gluten-free flours. I have tested most of these flours and selected a few based on how light and fluffy they make a sponge cake and whether they are accessible and affordable. My favorite gluten-free flours are as follows:

Fine white rice flour is a light flour. Compared to other gluten-free flours, it creates a fluffy and delicate baked treat. It also has minimal taste, allowing the other ingredients to shine. Make sure that you purchase *fine* white rice flour rather than *coarse* white rice flour for baking. I find that brown rice flour is a little grittier than white rice flour, and it does not create fluffy cakes, but some people cannot tell the difference.

Almond meal adds moisture to baked treats, and it gives your baked treat a beautiful crumb that just melts in your mouth!

Premade gluten-free baking blends, unlike individual gluten-free flours, have added gums to help create stability in your baked treat. Many blends have a bland taste, so they have minimal impact on the flavor of the treat. They can be a little inconsistent and temperamental though, so I have used them to a minimum.

I also love quinoa flour and banana flour because they help create fluffy and moist baked goods. However, they both impart a nutty or earthy taste so are best for more wholesome loaves and muffins. They can also be quite costly!

SWEETENERS

Most of the recipes in this book have an unrefined natural sweeteners option. The sweeteners that I use include the following:

Dates. Unlike other sweeteners, dates are packed with fiber, which slows down the digestion of sugar. I often use dates in unbaked cake bases because they help the nuts and seeds stick together. I love snacking on fresh Medjool dates, but I mostly use dried Deglet Noor dates in my recipes as they are more affordable.

Coconut sugar. I love using coconut sugar in baked cakes. Its granulated and dry texture allows cakes to rise well and become fluffy. Granulated sugar is often used in baked treats to give them structure. Dates and liquid sweeteners will weigh down baked treats, resulting in a denser texture.

Rice malt syrup, maple syrup, and coconut nectar. I use liquid sweeteners when I need ingredients to stick together or to sweeten "wet" recipes such as cheesecakes. I use rice malt syrup as it is the most affordable, but I love the taste of maple syrup and coconut nectar. Note that rice malt syrup is less sweet than other liquid sweeteners, so feel free to adjust the amount of sweetener in these recipes to your liking.

I use white granulated sugar in a couple of recipes as many unrefined sweeteners darken or weigh down the texture of a baked treat. I'm lucky that white sugar processed in Australia is vegan. However, in some countries, white sugar is not fully vegan as it has been bleached using animal bones. If this is a concern for you, purchase organic raw sugar or an unrefined sweetener.

HOW TO MAKE DESSERTS FOR PEOPLE WITH SPECIFIC ALLERGIES AND SENSITIVITIES

—

Nuts. Many of the recipes in this book contain nuts. If you avoid nuts, there is no single replacement so here are a few options:

In some recipes such as the granola, you can simply omit them or substitute seeds such as sunflower and pumpkin. Nut butters can be substituted for sunflower seed butter.

I use almond meal in my gluten-free baked recipes to ensure they are moist and have a texture that is similar to treats with gluten. However, due to the fat content of almond meal, it cannot be replaced 1:1 with other flours without additional amendments. If you can eat gluten, I have made recommendations in a few recipes on how to substitute almond meal with plain wheat flour.

The cashews in the unbaked cakes and cashew buttercream can be substituted with soaked sunflower seeds. If the flavor is too earthy for you, add a dollop of plant-based yogurt to balance out the taste. Note that sunflower seeds will make the "cream" a light brown color. If you cannot eat cashews but are fine with other nuts, macadamia nuts can be used instead.

Soy. I have used soymilk in some recipes, but you can substitute your milk of choice.

Coconut. There is no single replacement for coconut but here are my suggestions:

I use coconut sugar in several recipes, but this can be substituted with any granulated sugar. If you want to make sure it is vegan, use organic granulated sugar.

For the unbaked cheesecakes, the coconut oil can be substituted with a smaller amount of cacao butter or vegetable shortening. The coconut cream can be substituted with a slightly smaller amount of silken tofu and extra fats. Experiment with proportions of ingredients until you find one where you like the texture and flavor. In unbaked cheesecake recipes, you cannot substitute coconut oil for a liquid vegetable oil as they do not set in the same way.

OTHER ESSENTIALS

There are a few other ingredients that I love using to make desserts:

Cashews. When raw cashews are combined with water and plant-based milk and cream, they make a creamy foundation for cheesecakes and sauces. In vegan desserts, cashews are used more often than other nuts because they have a subtler taste, are softer, and are easily blended.

Raw cacao powder. Raw cacao powder has not been heated above 113°F (45°C), and it has several nutritional properties such as being high in magnesium and antioxidants. This is different from cocoa powder, which has been processed at high temperatures, causing it to lose many of its nutrients. (This was identified in the *Journal of Agriculture and Food Chemistry.*) Most supermarket and bakery treats use the latter, cocoa powder.

Ground cinnamon. I love adding cinnamon to my treats as it has a natural sweet tone and it adds complexity to desserts.

I live by the philosophy that breakfast is the most important—and delicious—meal of the day! My days are unpredictable and work can be busier than expected, so I always make sure I have a tasty and satiating breakfast that fills me up until lunchtime.

——

This chapter includes simple breakfasts that you can prepare the night before, cute breakfasts for kids, and indulgent breakfasts inspired by desserts . . . because life is too short to skip dessert. I love eating these dishes in the morning, but nothing can stop you from enjoying these recipes at any time of the day!

Good morning!

NOURISHING BREAKFASTS

OVERNIGHT OATS: THREE WAYS!

YIELD: 2 SERVINGS PER RECIPE

Overnight oats is a quick and simple breakfast that you can prepare the night before! It is ideal for those who struggle to get out of bed (me) or who don't have time in the morning to prepare breakfast. Pop the oats in a lidded jar so you can have it on your way to work or school! The chia seeds make the oats super creamy without having to stand at the stove like cooking traditional porridge.

BLUEBERRY AND BANANA BREAD

1½ cups (355 ml) plant-based milk, such as almond, soy, or coconut

1 cup (96 g) rolled oats

2 tablespoons (26 g) chia seeds

1 medium-size banana (about 4 ounces, or 120 g), peeled

½ teaspoon ground cinnamon

1 cup (145 g) fresh blueberries

APPLE PIE

1½ cups (355 ml) plant-based milk, such as almond, soy, or coconut

1 cup (96 g) rolled oats

2 tablespoons (26 g) chia seeds

½ teaspoon ground cinnamon

1 medium-size apple (about 6½ ounces, or 180 g), chopped and stewed

¾ cup (about 80 g) Whatever-you-want Date-Sweetened Granola (page 27)

PEANUT BUTTER AND JAM

1½ cups (355 ml) plant-based milk, such as almond, soy, or coconut

1 cup (96 g) rolled oats

2 tablespoons (26 g) chia seeds

½ cup (65 g) fresh raspberries

¼ cup (65 g) smooth or crunchy peanut butter

½ recipe Raspberry Chia Jam (page 139)

1} The night before, combine the milk, oats, and chia seeds in a lidded container or large jar.

2} For the blueberry and banana oats, mash the banana, and mix it into the oats with the cinnamon. For the apple pie oats, mix the cinnamon into the oats.

3} Store in the fridge overnight. The next morning, mix the oats again to ensure everything is evenly distributed. Arrange the oats and the remaining ingredients in 2 bowls or jars. Enjoy!

TIP

Feel free to sweeten your oats with any additional sweetener!

TIP

_For the smoothie bowl
recipes, if you prefer thick
smoothies, use less milk
and process the ingredients
in a food processor._

My favorite breakfast in the warmer seasons is a nourishing bowl of plant-based yogurt or a smoothie topped with a ridiculous amount of granola! The smoothies have a texture similar to thick shakes or soft-serve ice cream, and they're taken to the next level with crunchy granola. It's fun to make bowls reminiscent of popular desserts by using certain ingredients and toppings.

BLISSFUL BREKKIE BOWLS

YIELD: EACH RECIPE SERVES 1

TROPICAL DREAMS

½ cup (about 85 g) plant-based yogurt, such as coconut, soy, or almond

¾ cup (about 80 g) Whatever-you-want Date-Sweetened Granola (page 27)

Sliced seasonal fruit such as nectarine or mango

1 passionfruit, pulp only (about 1 ounce, or 35 g)

1 piece of dried pineapple

1 tablespoon (4 g) flaked coconut

Add all the ingredients to a bowl and enjoy immediately.

PINK DRAGON FRUIT FUN

½ medium-size banana (about 2 ounces, or 60 g), peeled and frozen

¼ medium-size pink dragon fruit (about 2 ounces, or 60 g), skin removed and frozen

1 cup (235 ml) plant-based milk, such as almond, soy, or coconut

¾ cup (about 80 g) Whatever-you-want Date-Sweetened Granola (page 27)

¼ cup (30 g) fresh strawberries, stems removed

1 fresh fig, sliced in quarters

1 tablespoon (8 g) pistachios, roughly chopped

1} Add the banana, dragon fruit, and milk to a blender. Blend until it is as smooth as possible.

2} Pour the smoothie into a bowl and top it with the granola, fruit, and pistachios. Enjoy immediately.

NOTELLA

1 medium-size banana (about 120 g), peeled and frozen

1 cup (235 ml) plant-based milk, such as almond, soy, or coconut

¼ cup (34 g) + 2 tablespoons (17 g) roasted or raw hazelnuts

1 tablespoon (5 g) cocoa or raw cacao powder

¼ cup (about 40 g) fresh berries or currants

¾ cup (about 80 g) Whatever-you-want Date-Sweetened Granola (page 27)

1 teaspoon cacao nibs

1} Add the banana, milk, ¼ cup (34 g) of hazelnuts, and cocoa powder to a blender. Blend until it is as smooth as possible.

2} Pour the smoothie into a bowl and top it with the remaining hazelnuts, fresh fruit, granola, and cacao nibs. Enjoy immediately.

WHATEVER-YOU-WANT DATE-SWEETENED GRANOLA

YIELD: 10 TO 20 SERVINGS

This granola is great in the morning with smoothies . . . or when you are feeling peckish throughout the day. I tend to eat it like a snack by the handful! I used dates to sweeten this granola as they're packed with fiber and give the granola a hint of caramel flavor. I often make granola using any bits and bobs leftover in my pantry so feel free to experiment with ingredients you already have! The oven temperature is relatively low as dates bake quickly (and burn) in the oven.

2 cups (320 g) pitted dates, soaked in water for at least 4 hours

½ cup (68 g) hazelnuts

½ cup (73 g) almonds

2 cups (192 g) rolled oats

2 cups (34 g) puffed brown rice

1 cup (184 g) raw buckwheat

½ cup (73 g) sunflower seeds

½ cup (69 g) pumpkin seeds

½ cup (75 g) hemp seeds

½ cup (30 g) flaked coconut

1 tablespoon (7 g) ground cinnamon

Pinch of salt

1} Preheat the oven to 300°F (150°C, or gas mark 2).

2} Thoroughly drain the dates and add them to a food processor. Process the dates until they form a paste and then add them to a large mixing bowl.

3} Add the hazelnuts and almonds to the food processor and pulse for 5 seconds or until the nuts form large chunks. Add the nuts and all the other ingredients to the large mixing bowl. Mix all the ingredients using your hands or with a spatula until the everything is evenly distributed. Spread the mixture on 2 lined baking trays.

4} Bake the granola in the oven for 25 minutes and then use a spatula or spoon to mix the granola to allow it to cook evenly. Bake for another 10 minutes or until all the granola is dry to the touch.

5} Remove the granola from oven and let it cool completely on the baking tray. Store in an airtight container at room temperature for up to 1 month or in the fridge for up to 2 months.

TIP

If you forgot to soak your dates, you can quickly soften them by soaking them in hot water for 5 to 10 minutes.

It's worthwhile to bake these oats just to make your home smell amazing! Baked oats are one of my more indulgent breakfasts even though it's so easy to prepare. The inside has a custard-like creaminess like stove-cooked oats, but the surface is crispy like the top of a crème brûlée! I like to prepare this the night before, pop it in the oven when I wake up, and get ready for the day. By the time I'm done (or properly wake up), I have a hot breakfast waiting for me.

APPLE AND BLUEBERRY PIE BAKED OATS

YIELD: 4 TO 6 SERVINGS

1 banana (about 4 ounces, or 120 g), mashed (optional), or ¼ cup (80 g) of your choice of sweetener (optional)

1⅔ cup (160 g) rolled oats

2 cups (475 ml) plant-based milk, such as almond, soy, or coconut

Dash of ground cinnamon

½ cup (75 g) blueberries

1 medium-size apple (about 6½ ounces, or 180 g), core removed and thinly sliced

1} The night before, add the banana or sweetener (if using), oats, and milk to a large container. Mix until combined. Set aside in the fridge.

2} Before you are ready to eat, preheat the oven to 350°F (180°C, or gas mark 4). Mix the blueberries into the oats. Pour the oats in an ovenproof dish and arrange the apple on top.

3} Bake the oats for 30 minutes or until the surface is slightly golden brown. Enjoy warm by itself or with plant-based milk or yogurt. The oats are best eaten fresh out of the oven, but leftovers can be stored in an airtight container in the fridge for up to 3 days.

These nut-free treats are really easy to make, and they can be packed with whatever ingredients you like! The dates are a wholesome natural sweetener, and when paired with a liquid sweetener, the dry ingredients stick together to form a slab of seedy goodness. These can be enjoyed on the go, such as on a hiking trip.

SUPER-SEEDY MUESLI BARS

YIELD: 8 BARS

½ cup (80 g) pitted dates, soaked in water for at least 4 hours

1 cup (96 g) rolled oats

½ cup (160 g) rice malt or maple syrup, or any other plant-based liquid sweetener

½ cup (92 g) raw buckwheat

½ cup (69 g) pumpkin seeds

½ cup (73 g) sunflower seeds

½ cup (9 g) puffed rice, (87 g) quinoa, (55 g) millet, or (52 g) amaranth

2 tablespoons (26 g) chia seeds

2 tablespoons (32 g) sunflower seed butter (optional)

1 teaspoon ground cinnamon (optional)

Pinch of salt

1} Preheat the oven to 325°F (160°C, or gas mark 3). Line an 8-inch (20 cm) square baking pan with parchment paper.

2} Drain the dates. Blend with a stick blender or food processor until it forms a paste. Add all of the ingredients to a medium-size mixing bowl and mix until everything is evenly combined. Scoop into the baking pan and firmly press down the mixture with the back of a spoon or cake scraper.

3} Bake in the oven for 25 to 30 minutes or until it turns golden brown. Let it completely cool in the baking pan.

4} Remove from the pan and use a sharp serrated knife or chef's knife to cut into bars. Use a gentle sawing action and hold the bars in place to minimize any crumbling.

5} Enjoy immediately or store in an airtight container at room temperature for 1 week, in the fridge for 2 weeks, or in the freezer for up to 2 months.

I have a tendency to burn food on the stovetop—so I created these pancakes to avoid burning my house down! I love baking these pancakes for breakfast or a quick late-night snack. Instead of using eggs as a binder and raising ingredient, the banana acts as a natural binder and the baking powder helps the pancakes to rise. The pancakes are naturally sweetened, so they are best served with nut butters and plain coconut yogurt. If you prefer thinner crepe-like pancakes, simply use more plant-based milk or water.

EASY BAKED BANANA PANCAKES

—

YIELD: 4 SMALL PANCAKES, 2 SERVINGS

2 cups (300 g) chunks of banana, roughly broken up by hand

1 cup (96 g) rolled oats

½ cup (120 ml) plant-based milk or water

1½ teaspoons baking powder

1} Preheat the oven to 350°F (180°C, or gas mark 4).

2} Add all the ingredients to a blender. Blend for around 15 seconds or until there are no more chunks of banana or whole pieces of rolled oats and everything is combined.

3} Pour the batter in circles on 1 or 2 lined baking trays. Bake for 15 to 18 minutes or until the pancakes can easily be removed from the tray. Make sure the bottoms of the pancakes are cooked and not wet. Enjoy immediately.

TIP

—

Feel free to get creative with the shape of these pancakes! The batter can be poured into cute animal shapes, which kids will love. Trust me, I've served these to kids and there were many shrieks of excitement! Make sure you adjust the baking time if you're making smaller pancakes. See the next page for some cute ideas!

FARM
FRESH
FERDINAND ZETTELMEY
76 WB.-NIEDERBAC
F. ZETTELMEYER
N. BACHEM
ORANGE
Freshly squeezed JUICE
FERDINAND ZETTELME
76 WB.-NI DERBACH

When I was doing university exchange in England, I lived with a French-speaking student from Belgium. We had turns making a dish from our country and she made French toast . . . and showed us the traditional way to make it! I put my own spin on French toast by using dense sourdough bread and serving it with caramelized peaches and a cashew cream for extra decadence.

PEACHES AND CREAM SOURDOUGH FRENCH TOAST

YIELD: 2 SERVINGS

1 cup (235 ml) plant-based milk, such as almond, soy, or coconut

2 tablespoons (26 g) chia seeds

1 teaspoon ground cinnamon

1 teaspoon vanilla extract

Pinch of black salt (optional)

4 slices of sourdough bread

2–4 peaches, sliced

Olive oil or vegan butter for cooking

Maple syrup

1 recipe Cashew Cream (page 149)

1} Add the milk, chia seeds, cinnamon, vanilla, and black salt (if using) to a blender. Blend until smooth and pour the mixture in a shallow bowl.

2} Dip each slice of bread in the mixture, allowing each slice to soak up the batter. Make sure all areas of the bread are covered in the batter.

3} Heat up a large saucepan over medium-high heat and drizzle with oil. Place the bread in the saucepan. Cook each side for 3 to 5 minutes or until golden brown. Set aside the bread in a warm spot.

4} Turn down the stove to medium heat. Drizzle oil in the saucepan and add the sliced peaches. When one side of the peaches begins to change color, drizzle some maple syrup over the slices and allow it to caramelize. Flip the peaches and allow the other side to caramelize.

5} Immediately serve the toast with the caramelized peaches and cashew cream. Drizzle with maple syrup as desired.

TIP

Black salt, or kala namak, is high in sodium chloride so it smells and tastes like eggs. It is often used in South Asian cooking and can be purchased from South Asian or Indian grocery stores.

These colorful treats are perfect for breakfast in the summer or as a snack on a hot day. Simply keep them in the freezer and grab one when you need to cool down! The granola's sweet crunchiness complements the smooth tanginess of the fruity yogurt. When you blend the fruit with the yogurt, the fruit's natural sugar and fiber prevents the yogurt from freezing into an ice brick, which makes the popsicles easier to devour. Feel free to experiment with different types of fruits!

RAINBOW FROZEN YOGURT GRANOLA POPSICLES

YIELD: 6 POPSICLES

¾ cup (about 80 g) Whatever-you-want Date-Sweetened Granola (page 27)

¼ cup (about 80 g) rice malt syrup or maple syrup, to taste

1 cup (about 170 g) plant-based yogurt, such as coconut, soy, or almond

¼ cup (about 36 g) blueberries

¼ cup (about 31 g) raspberries

¼ cup (about 44 g) chopped mango

1} Mix the granola and half of the sweetener in a small bowl. Scoop the mixture into the popsicle molds and firmly press them down.

2} Mix the remaining sweetener with the yogurt and divide it between 3 small bowls. Add the blueberries to one bowl, raspberries to the second bowl, and mango to the third bowl. Use a stick blender to blend the fruit with the yogurt. Scoop the yogurt into the popsicle molds; each bowl should have enough yogurt for 2 popsicles. Set the popsicles aside in the freezer.

3} Freeze the popsicles for 4 hours or until completely firm. Enjoy straight from the freezer.

Snack time

IS ANY TIME!

*Let's be real: We don't always want to
spend hours in the kitchen preparing food.*

—

*This chapter provides recipes that you can make quickly
and freeze for whenever you need a snack.
The ingredients are safe at room temperature, or they
have been prepared or baked in a way that allows some of them
to be stored at room temperature for around three days.
Many of these treats are ideal for bringing to work,
school, or for packing in your child's lunch box. I always
make sure I have snacks on hand as life shouldn't
be spent feeling hangry!*

BLISS BALLS, THREE WAYS!

YIELD: 8 TO 12 BLISS BALLS OF EACH FLAVOR

Bliss balls are a great introduction to unbaked treats as they are super easy and quick to make! These balls can be kept at room temperature for a couple of days, which makes them the perfect snack for road trips or work/study days. There are so many different sweeteners, nuts, and seeds that you can combine to make different taste sensations and experiences. I've listed some of my favorite combinations for you! If you don't have a food processor, try to purchase the ground version of the nut and seed and combine it with chopped Medjool dates or a liquid sweetener.

CHOCOLATE-HAZELNUT BALLS

1½ cups (203 g) raw or roasted hazelnuts

½ cup (80 g) pitted dates, soaked in water for at least 4 hours

3 tablespoons (15 g) raw cacao powder or cocoa, to taste

Pinch of salt

TROPICAL BLISS BALLS

1⅓ cup (113 g) desiccated coconut

¾ cup (105 g) raw or roasted cashews

½ packed cup (60 g) dried unsweetened mango and pineapple, soaked in water for at least 4 hours

Pinch of salt

1 slice of dried unsweetened mango or pineapple (optional)

Pinch of turmeric powder (optional)

CHERRY COCONUT BALLS

1⅓ cup (193 g) raw or roasted almonds

½ cup (80 g) dried cherries, soaked in water for at least 4 hours

Pinch of salt

3 tablespoons (21 g) almond meal, for coating

Pinch of beetroot, berry, or pink dragon fruit powder

To make the chocolate-hazelnut: Add the hazelnuts to a food processor and process until it forms small crumbs. Reserve a handful of the crumbs for later. Drain the dates and add them to the processor with the cacao powder and salt. Process until the mixture comes together. Roll the mixture into balls and roll in the reserved hazelnut crumbs.

To make the tropical bliss: Reserve a handful of the coconut for decorating. Add the coconut and cashews to a food processor and process until it forms small crumbs. Drain the mango and pineapple, add them to the processor with the salt, and process until the mixture comes together. Finely chop the remaining slice of mango or pineapple (if using) and toss in a small bowl with the reserved coconut and turmeric (if using). Roll the mixture into balls and roll in the golden coconut mixture.

To make the cherry coconut: Add the almonds to a food processor and process until it forms small crumbs. Drain the cherries, add them to the processor with the salt, and process until the mixture combines. Mix the almond meal and beetroot powder in a small bowl. Roll the mixture into balls and roll in the pink almond mixture.

Store the bliss balls in an airtight container at room temperature for up to 1 day, in the fridge for up to 1 week, or in the freezer for up to 2 months.

TIP

If any of the mixtures are too dry, add a splash of water or coconut oil and then process until it comes together.

Lamingtons are a classic Australian bakery treat where two vanilla sponge cakes sandwich a sweet layer of jam, are covered in chocolate, and dipped in coconut. Unlike the classic treat, these lamingtons are vegan, bite-sized, and wholesome! This recipe features a whole raspberry encased by an unbaked cashew and coconut "sponge" dipped in chocolate and coconut. They are fun to eat because you get a burst of flavors with every bite. It is one of the most popular recipes on my website, and I have received rave reviews from my website readers, customers, family, and friends.

DECADENT RAW LAMINGTON BLISS BALLS

—

YIELD: 10 BLISS BALLS

BLISS BALL MIXTURE

1 cup (140 g) cashews

⅓ cup (28 g) desiccated coconut

¼ cup (80 g) rice malt or maple syrup, or any other plant-based liquid sweetener

2 tablespoons (28 g) coconut oil

½ cup (65 g) fresh or (70 g) frozen whole raspberries (Frozen is easier.)

COATING

1 cup (180 g) store-bought vegan chocolate, roughly chopped OR

⅓ cup (75 g) cacao butter, chopped

⅓ cup (27 g) raw cacao powder or cocoa powder

2 tablespoons (40 g) rice malt or maple syrup, or any other plant-based liquid sweetener to taste

2 tablespoons (28 g) coconut oil

2 tablespoons (28 ml) coconut cream

½ cup (43 g) desiccated coconut

TIP

When coating the balls in chocolate and coconut, avoid getting the chocolate all over your hands (and face) by allowing the excess chocolate to drip through the fork, placing it in the shallow dish of coconut, and tossing coconut around the ball so you don't have to touch the wet chocolate.

1} **To make the bliss ball mixture:** Add the cashews and coconut to a food processor. Process until it forms small crumbs. Add the rice malt syrup and coconut oil and process until combined.

2} Using wet hands, gently wrap about 2 tablespoons (about 30 g) of the bliss ball mixture around each raspberry, making sure there are no gaps; otherwise, the raspberry may leak. Place the balls on a lined plate or tray and set aside in the freezer.

3} **To make the chocolate:** If you have store-bought chocolate, gently melt it in a small saucepan or in a double boiler over low heat. If you are making your own chocolate, melt the cacao butter, cacao powder, and sweetener in the same way. Add the coconut oil and coconut cream to the melted chocolate and use a whisk or a stick blender to fully emulsify the mixture so the oils are fully combined with the rest of the ingredients.

4} Place the desiccated coconut in a shallow bowl. When the balls are firm to the touch, remove them from the freezer. Using a fork, quickly dip each ball in the chocolate and then toss them in the coconut. Return the balls to the freezer for at least 10 minutes to allow the chocolate to set.

5} Store the bliss balls in an airtight container at room temperature for 1 day, in the fridge for up to 5 days, or in the freezer for up to 1 month.

There's something so satisfying about biting into chocolate and being surprised by an oozing filling! These are a great movie snack as the chocolate and fillings are stable at room temperature, or they can be enjoyed with a cup of tea as an afternoon pick-me-up. Feel free to experiment with fillings—for example you can substitute peppermint extract with rose water to create a Turkish-inspired treat.

CHOCOLATE CUPS, THREE WAYS

YIELD: 12 MINI CHOCOLATE CUPS

CHOCOLATE CUPS

1 recipe DIY Chocolate (page 140) or 1⅓ cups (250 g) store-bought vegan chocolate

SUNFLOWER BUTTER AND JAM FILLING

½ cup (130 g) sunflower seed butter or any nut butter

½ cup (95 g) Raspberry Chia Jam (page 139)

TAHINI CARAMEL FILLING

12 pitted Medjool dates

¾ cup (175 ml) water

Pinch of salt

2 tablespoons (30 g) tahini or (32 g) any nut butter

MINT COCONUT FILLING

½ cup (112 g) coconut butter

½ cup (43 g) desiccated coconut

1 tablespoon (20 g) rice malt syrup, maple syrup, or any plant-based liquid sweetener to taste

2–3 drops of peppermint extract

1} Melt the chocolate in a small saucepan or double boiler over low heat. When the chocolate has fully melted, remove it from the heat.

2} Allow the chocolate to cool until it is the consistency of thin cream or it leaves a "ribbon" when you drizzle it. Pour about 1 teaspoon of chocolate into a small silicon cup. Gently rotate the cup or use the back of a spoon to coat the sides of the cup with chocolate. Make sure the bottom and sides are covered in adequate chocolate; otherwise, the cup will break. Repeat for the remaining cups and set aside in the freezer.

3} **To make the tahini caramel filling:** Use a blender to puree all the ingredients until they are as smooth as possible.

To make the mint coconut filling: Mix all the ingredients in a small bowl.

4} Remove the chocolate cups from the freezer. If the sides are too thin, add more chocolate to the area and freeze again. When the cups are ready, scoop your choice of filling into the cup, leaving a little space at the top for more chocolate. Cover each cup with the remaining melted chocolate, decorate if desired, and then set aside in the fridge or freezer.

5} When the cups are firm to the touch, carefully remove each one from their mold. Enjoy immediately or store in an airtight container at room temperature for 1 day, in the fridge for 1 week, or in the freezer for up to 2 months.

Here's an easy recipe that can be made and decorated with kids as young as three years old! The cookies are crisp on the outside and soft in the middle. The addition of cinnamon makes them smell and taste so homey that adults will want to bake these for themselves! Don't be intimidated by using avocado in the frosting—the avocado makes an extremely creamy (and healthy) frosting and the taste is masked by the cocoa and sweetener. Just make sure you blend it up well; otherwise, it will look and taste unappetizing.

BEAR-FRIENDLY CINNAMON COOKIES

———

YIELD: 12 ANIMAL-FACE COOKIES
WITH NOSES

COOKIES

2 cups (250 g) all-purpose flour

1 cup (144 g) coconut sugar

1 tablespoon (7 g) ground cinnamon

½ teaspoon baking soda

1 teaspoon vanilla extract or vanilla bean powder

½ cup (120 ml) light-tasting vegetable oil, such as sunflower

3–6 tablespoons (45–90 ml) plant-based milk, such as almond, soy, or coconut, as needed

FROSTING

1 avocado, pitted and skin removed

¼ cup (20 g) cocoa or raw cacao powder

5 pitted Medjool dates or ½ cup (72 g) coconut sugar, to taste

DECORATIONS

Fresh blueberries

Vegan chocolate and white chocolate buds

Dried fruit

1} Preheat the oven to 350°F (180°C, or gas mark 4).

2} **To make the cookies:** Add all the dry cookie ingredients to a large bowl. Mix until combined and there are no lumps. Add the wet ingredients and mix until it forms a dough. Add more milk if the dough isn't coming together. The dough should be an even color, pliable, and come together in a large ball.

3} To make smaller cookies (for the noses of the animals), grab a handful of the dough. Pinch about 1 teaspoon of the dough, roll into balls, and flatten. Place on a lined baking tray. To make larger cookies (for the faces of the animals), use the remaining dough. Pinch about 1½ tablespoons (about 25 g) of the dough, roll into balls, and flatten. Place the cookies on a separate lined baking tray.

4} Bake the smaller cookies for about 6 minutes and the larger cookies for about 10 to 12 minutes. The cookies are ready when they turn golden brown.

5} **To make the frosting:** Add all the ingredients to a small bowl. Use a stick blender to blend until it is as smooth as possible and you cannot see any lumps of avocado. Decorate the cookies as desired!

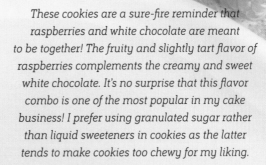

These cookies are a sure-fire reminder that raspberries and white chocolate are meant to be together! The fruity and slightly tart flavor of raspberries complements the creamy and sweet white chocolate. It's no surprise that this flavor combo is one of the most popular in my cake business! I prefer using granulated sugar rather than liquid sweeteners in cookies as the latter tends to make cookies too chewy for my liking.

RASPBERRY AND WHITE CHOCOLATE COOKIES

YIELD: 12 TO 15 COOKIES

DRY INGREDIENTS

1¼ cup (200 g) white rice flour or all-purpose flour

1¼ cup (140 g) almond meal

½ cup (72 g) coconut sugar

½ cup (112 g) white chocolate chips or chopped white chocolate

½ teaspoon baking soda

Pinch of salt

WET INGREDIENTS

⅓ cup (80 ml) light-tasting vegetable oil, such as sunflower

3 tablespoons (45 ml) aquafaba

2–4 tablespoons (28–60 ml) plant-based milk, such as almond, soy, or coconut, as needed

½ cup (70 g) frozen or (65 g) fresh raspberries

1} Preheat the oven to 350°F (180°C, or gas mark 4).

2} Add all the dry ingredients to a large mixing bowl. Mix until combined and there are no lumps except from the white chocolate. Add the oil, aquafaba, and milk and mix until it forms a dough. Add more milk if the dough isn't coming together. The dough should be soft and pliable. Gently fold the raspberries into the cookie dough.

3} Take about 1½ tablespoons (about 25 g) of cookie dough at a time, roll into balls, and flatten on a lined baking tray, leaving some space between the cookies. Repeat until all the dough has been used up.

4} Bake the cookies for 12 to 15 minutes or until the edges are golden brown. Cool on a wire rack and enjoy them warm. When the cookies are completely cool, store them in an airtight container. They can be stored in the fridge for up to 1 week or in the freezer for up to 1 month.

NOTES

These cookies will soften over time. To make the cookies crispy again, pop them on a lined baking tray in the oven at 210°F (100°C) for 5 minutes. When they cool, they will crisp up. Cookies with a longer shelf life tend to have a high proportion of fats and sugars, but I kept both amounts relatively low to keep them wholesome!

For nut-free cookies, substitute both flours with 1¾ cup (219 g) all-purpose flour and increase the oil to ½ cup (120 ml).

TIP

Make ice cream sandwiches by sandwiching two cookies with a scoop of ice cream, such as on page 52!

CHOCOLATE BROWNIE PEANUT BUTTER SANDWICH COOKIES

Oh my, oh my, these brownie cookies—or brookies—are divine! A crispy and chewy cookie exterior envelopes the most heavenly and fudgy brownie and a peanut butter filling. The brownie cookies are pretty decadent, so you could also have them without the peanut butter filling. The almond meal gives the brownies moisture, which is sooo important for any epic dessert. I used coconut flour in the filling to firm up the peanut butter so it doesn't melt at room temperature, but you can omit the flour and use straight up peanut butter.

YIELD: 10 TO 12 BROWNIE COOKIE
SANDWICHES

BROWNIE COOKIES

1 cup (144 g) coconut sugar

1¼ cup (140 g) almond meal

¾ cup (120 g) white rice flour or (94 g) all-purpose flour

⅓ cup (27 g) cocoa powder or raw cacao powder

1 tablespoon (13 g) chia seeds or (12 g) flaxseeds, ground

½ teaspoon baking powder

Pinch of salt

¼ cup (60 ml) light-tasting vegetable oil, such as sunflower

⅓ cup (80 ml) plant-based milk, such as almond, soy, or coconut

PEANUT BUTTER FILLING

¾ cup (195 g) smooth or chunky peanut butter

¼ cup (28 g) coconut flour

Maple, rice malt syrup, or any other plant-based liquid sweetener, to taste

1} Preheat the oven to 350°F (180°C, or gas mark 4).

2} **To make the cookies:** Add all the brownie cookie dry ingredients to a medium-size bowl. Mix until combined and there are no lumps. Add the wet ingredients to the bowl and mix and squeeze with your hands until combined. The mixture should be pliable enough to be rolled into balls. Add a splash of milk if necessary.

3} Grab about 2 tablespoons (about 30 g) of the batter, roll into balls, and flatten on a lined baking tray. Leave some space in between the cookies for spreading. Bake in the oven for 10 to 12 minutes or until the brownie cookies are dry to the touch. Allow them to cool on the baking tray and to set further.

4} **To make the peanut butter filling:** Add all the ingredients to a small bowl and mix until combined. The filling should be like a wet dough.

5} **To assemble:** Scoop the peanut butter filling on top of half of the brownie cookies. Sandwich the filling with the remainder of the brownie cookies.

6} Store in an airtight container at room temperature for up to 3 days, in the fridge for 1 week, or in the freezer for up to 1 month.

TIP

If you don't already have ground chia seeds or flaxseeds, combine them in a blender with the wet ingredients and blend. It can be difficult to grind the seeds by themselves so it's easier to blend them with lots of liquids.

For nut-free brownie cookies, substitute both flours with 1⅓ cup (167 g) all-purpose flour and increase the oil to ⅓ cup (80 ml). Use sunflower butter instead of peanut butter in the filling.

WHOLESOME CRISPY RICE ROCKY ROAD BARS

I loved going to the chocolate shop as a kid and picking my own treats to share with my family... or hide in my secret stash at home! These bars are inspired by one of my favorite treats: rocky road. I took the flavors and textures of rocky road such as the sweet bursts of jelly, fluffy marshmallow, and crunchy nuts and then simplified them for this recipe. I bulked it up with brown rice puffs, which makes it "healthy" enough to eat in the morning, right?! You only need one bowl and a container to make this easy treat!

YIELD: ABOUT 10 VERY LARGE BARS

2½ cups (450 g) roughly chopped vegan chocolate

2 tablespoons (28 g) cacao butter or (28 ml) any vegetable oil

2 cups (34 g) brown rice puffs

½ cup (62 g) raw or roasted pistachios

½ cup (73 g) raw or roasted almonds

¼ cup (30 g) dried cranberries

¼ cup (40 g) goji berries

½ cup (30 g) flaked coconut

Rose petals, to decorate

TIP

Feel free to experiment with other nuts, seeds, and dried fruit. For a nut-free treat, substitute the nuts with roasted sunflower or pumpkin seeds!

1} Line a large loaf pan with parchment paper, ensuring the paper comes up the sides. I used an 11 × 5-inch (28 × 13 cm) pan, but any cake pan or container will do.

2} Add the chocolate and cacao butter or oil directly to a small saucepan or in a double boiler over medium heat. Gently stir for 5 minutes or until fully melted. Alternatively, melt the ingredients in a microwave at 15–30 second increments and mix until fully melted.

3} Add all the brown rice puffs, nuts, fruit, and coconut to a large bowl. Mix until they are roughly combined.

4} Pour the melted chocolate into the large bowl and mix until all the ingredients are evenly distributed. Scoop the mixture into lined loaf pan and press down the surface to ensure it is mostly flat. Sprinkle the rose petals on top. Set aside in the fridge for 3 hours or until firm.

5} Pull on the sides of the parchment paper to remove from the pan. Cut with a sharp knife. Enjoy immediately or store in an airtight container at room temperature for up to 1 week, in the fridge for up to 1 month, or in the freezer for up to 2 months.

COOKIE DOUGH BARS

—

YIELD: ABOUT 10 VERY LARGE BARS
OR 30 BITE-SIZED PIECES

COOKIE DOUGH

1 cup (96 g) rolled oats

1 heaped cup (approximately 240 g) of cooked chickpeas (or whatever amount of chickpeas you can get from a 14½ ounce [400 g] can)

¾ cup (195 g) cashew butter

¼ cup (80 g) maple or rice malt syrup, or any other plant-based liquid sweetener

1 teaspoon vanilla extract or vanilla bean powder

½ teaspoon salt

Plant-based milk or water, as needed

1 cup (180 g) roughly chopped vegan chocolate or chocolate chips

CHOCOLATE TOPPING

1 recipe thin Chocolate Ganache (page 143)

1} Line a large loaf pan with parchment paper, ensuring the paper comes up the sides. I used an 11 × 5-inch (28 × 13 cm) pan, but any cake pan or container will do.

2} Add the rolled oats to a food processor and process for 3 minutes or until it forms fine crumbs. Add the chickpeas, cashew butter, syrup, vanilla, and salt and process until it forms a paste. If the mixture is dry, add a little plant-based milk or water. Process until it forms a fudgy consistency. Remove the blade from the food processor and mix in the chocolate until evenly distributed.

3} Scoop the mixture into the pan and press down to make sure there are no gaps. Smooth the top with a spatula or cake scraper. Set aside.

4} Make the chocolate ganache according to the instructions. While the ganache is warm, pour it onto the cookie dough, making sure it is flat. Set it aside in the fridge for 4 hours or until set.

5} Remove from the fridge and pull on the sides of the parchment paper to remove. Cut with a sharp knife. Store in an airtight container at room temperature for a few hours, in the fridge for up to 3 days, or in the freezer up to 1 month.

TIP

If you don't have cashew butter, you can substitute it with roasted cashews. Just process them in your food processor with the rolled oats until it forms fine crumbs and then continue with the recipe.

*Many vegan ice cream recipes ask that you
defrost the ice cream before you eat it. However, when
I want ice cream, I don't want to wait for it!
To avoid this, I used a selective combination of
ingredients in these popsicles to prevent the popsicles
from freezing rock hard. Due to the high fiber and
natural oils in dates and nut butter, they never
completely freeze so you can eat them
straight from the freezer.*

CHOCOLATE FUDGSICLES

YIELD: 4 POPSICLES

POPSICLES

½ cup (80 g) pitted dates,
soaked in water for 2 hours

½ cup (130 g) almond butter

½ cup (120 ml) coconut cream

¼ cup (60 ml) plant-based milk,
such as almond, soy, or coconut

3 tablespoons (15 g) cocoa
or raw cacao powder

COATING

½ cup DIY Chocolate (page 140)
or ⅔ cup (125 g) store-bought
vegan chocolate

½ cup (50 g) chopped almonds
or other nuts

1} Drain the dates. Add them to a high-powered blender
with all the popsicle ingredients. Blend until the mixture is
as smooth as possible.

2} Spoon the mixture into your popsicle molds and place
sticks in the popsicles. Freeze for at least 4 hours or until
the popsicles are frozen solid.

3} Remove the popsicles from their molds and store them in
an airtight container.

4} Melt the chocolate in a small saucepan or over a double
boiler. Quickly spoon the chocolate over each popsicle
and decorate as desired. The temperature of the popsicles
will set the chocolate straight away. Enjoy the popsicles
immediately or store them in an airtight container in the
freezer for up to 2 months.

APPLE CHAI MUFFINS WITH A MAPLE GLAZE

YIELD: 12 TO 16 MUFFINS,
DEPENDING ON THE SIZE OF YOUR PAN

These wholesome muffins are amazing fresh from the oven or heated up, especially on a chilly day. Every bite is like a warm and caring hug! I love baking with apples as they have a subtle natural sweetness and pair well with cinnamon and chai, which are my favorite spices. The apples give the muffins moisture, which minimizes the need for extra oil or vegan butter.

DRY INGREDIENTS FOR MUFFINS

2 cups (224 g) blanched almond meal

1½ cups (240 g) white rice flour or (188 g) all-purpose flour

¾ cup (108 g) coconut sugar

½ cup pecans (50 g), roughly chopped

2 tablespoons (16 g) chai spice mix

1 tablespoon (14 g) baking powder

WET INGREDIENTS FOR MUFFINS

2 medium-size apples (about 13 ounces, or 360 g), cores removed

1⅓ cup (315 ml) plant-based milk, such as almond, soy, or coconut

½ cup (120 ml) light-tasting vegetable oil, such as sunflower

1 tablespoon (15 ml) apple cider vinegar or regular vinegar

MAPLE GLAZE

¼ cup (56 g) coconut butter

2–3 tablespoons (28–45 ml) plant-based milk, such as almond, soy, or coconut

2 tablespoons (40 g) maple syrup

1} Preheat the oven to 350°F (180°C, or gas mark 3).

2} In a large-size bowl, combine the dry ingredients and mix until combined.

3} Coarsely grate half of the apples and chop the other half into small pieces (about ¼-inch [6 mm] cubes). Add the apple and the rest of the wet ingredients to the bowl and mix until evenly combined. The mixture should be the consistency of thick pancake batter. Mix in more milk if the mixture is too thick.

4} Scoop the batter into lined muffin pans, filling each very close to the top.

5} Bake the muffins for 25 to 30 minutes or until a skewer can be inserted into the center of a muffin and it comes out clean. Cool the muffins on a wire rack.

6} **To make the maple glaze:** If the coconut butter is solid, gently melt it in a small saucepan over low heat and then remove. Stir the milk and maple syrup into the coconut butter until they are fully combined. The glaze should be a consistency where it can be drizzled. If it is too thick, stir in more milk until it reaches the desired consistency. Drizzle the glaze over the muffins.

7} The muffins are best eaten the day they are baked. However, you can store them in an airtight container at room temperature for 3 days, in the fridge up to 1 week, or in the freezer for up to a month. Warm up the muffins before you eat them.

NOTE
These muffins can be made with regular wheat flour. Simply substitute both flours in the recipe with 3 cups (375 g) of all-purpose flour.

TIP

To make the chai spice mix: Use a blender or coffee grinder to blend whole chai tea leaves and spices into a fine powder. I keep a small jar of chai spices in my pantry so I can quickly add it to smoothies or cakes whenever I need!

These are muffins that are not too sweet—and a wholesome treat for adults and children alike! Gluten-free vegan baking is notoriously difficult, but this recipe makes it a breeze. Fine white rice flour and the natural oils in almond meal allow these muffins to be fluffy and moist. The lemon helps "tenderize" or soften the gluten-free flours, which gives the muffins a delicate crumb.

BLUEBERRY LEMON MUFFINS WITH A COCONUT CRUMBLE

YIELD: 12 TO 16 MUFFINS, DEPENDING ON THE SIZE OF YOUR PAN

CRUMBLE

¼ cup (40 g) white rice flour or (31 g) all-purpose flour

½ cup (40 g) shredded coconut

2 tablespoons (40 g) rice malt or maple syrup, or any other plant-based liquid sweetener

DRY INGREDIENTS FOR MUFFINS

1½ cups (240 g) white rice flour or (188 g) all-purpose flour

1½ cups (168 g) blanched almond meal

¾ cup (108 g) coconut sugar

2 teaspoons baking powder

WET INGREDIENTS FOR MUFFINS

1½ cups (355 ml) plant-based milk, such as almond, soy, or coconut

1 cup (145 g) fresh or (155 g) frozen blueberries

½ cup (120 ml) light-tasting vegetable oil, such as sunflower

2 tablespoons (28 ml) lemon juice and zest (about 1 lemon)

1} Preheat the oven to 350°F (180°C, or gas mark 3).

2} **To make the crumble:** In a medium-size bowl, add all the ingredients. Mix with your fingertips until crumbly and thoroughly combined. Set aside.

3} **To make the muffins:** In a large-size bowl, combine the dry ingredients. Mix until evenly combined and there are no lumps. Add the wet ingredients and mix until just combined or until there are no more lumps of flour. If you are in a warm climate, the muffin batter may be a little runny, but this is fine.

4} Scoop the muffin batter into lined muffin pans, filling each very close to the top. Sprinkle the crumble on top of the muffins.

5} Bake the muffins for 25 to 30 minutes or until a skewer can be inserted into the center of a muffin and it comes out clean. Cool the muffins on a wire rack.

6} The muffins are best eaten the day they are baked. However, you can store them in an airtight container at room temperature for 3 days, in the fridge up to 1 week, or in the freezer for up to a month. Warm up the muffins before you eat them.

TIP

These muffins can be made with regular flour. Substitute both flours in the recipe for 2⅔ cups (333 g) all-purpose flour and add an extra 1 tablespoon (15 ml) of oil.

BAKED CINNAMON DONUTS WITH A STRAWBERRY GLAZE

Classic donuts are characterized by their subtle cinnamon and nutmeg flavor and their sweet glaze, which is dry to the touch and "cracks" when you bite into it. I've replicated all those elements in this recipe! The oven temperature for this recipe is higher than usual as the donuts need to develop a crust so they can easily pop out of their molds. When making the glaze, I reduced the strawberries on the stove top to intensify their flavor and color. The frosting turns into a playful pastel pink color that reminds me of childhood!

YIELD: 18 DONUTS

DRY INGREDIENTS
2½ cups (300 g) self-rising flour

1¼ cups (250 g) white or (180 g) coconut sugar

1 tablespoon (13 g) chia seeds or (12 g) flaxseeds, ground

1½ teaspoons baking powder

1 teaspoon ground cinnamon

¼ teaspoon ground nutmeg

WET INGREDIENTS
1¼ cup (285 ml) plant-based milk, such as almond, soy, or coconut

¾ cup (175 ml) light-tasting vegetable oil, such as sunflower

1 tablespoon (15 ml) apple cider vinegar

PINK STRAWBERRY FROSTING AND DECORATION
1 cup (145 g) strawberries, stems removed

½ cup (112 g) refined coconut oil or vegetable shortening

3-4 cups (360–480 g) powdered sugar, as needed

3 tablespoons (45 ml) plant-based milk, such as almond, soy, or coconut

Sprinkles of choice

1} Preheat the oven to 375°F (190°C, or gas mark 5). If you have silicone donut trays, place them on a baking tray. If you have an aluminum donut tray, thoroughly grease it with oil.

2} Add all the dry ingredients to a large mixing bowl. Mix until combined and there are no lumps. Add the wet ingredients to the bowl and mix until just combined.

3} Spoon or pipe the batter into your donut trays, filling each mold about ¾ full. Bake the donuts for 13 to 15 minutes or until they are slightly golden brown. Let the donuts completely cool in the molds. If you try to remove the donuts earlier, they may crumble or stick to the molds. Remove the donuts and place them on a wire rack.

4} **To make the frosting:** Add the strawberries and a splash of water to a medium saucepan over high heat. Boil until the strawberries have completely broken down and can easily be smashed with the back of a fork. Puree with a stick blender and reduce the stove to medium-low heat. Add the oil or shortening and mix until it melts. Add the sugar and milk and then mix until everything is fully combined. When the frosting is warm, it should be a little thicker than a liquid sweetener. If it is too thick, add more milk. If it is too thin, add more powdered sugar. Remove from the heat.

5} **To decorate:** Spoon the frosting over each donut and sprinkle the decorations on top. Set aside for 10 to 15 minutes until the frosting sets and is dry to the touch.

6} Enjoy immediately or store in an airtight container at room temperature for 3 days, in the fridge for 5 days, or in the freezer up to 1 month.

TIP

For an easy way to grind up the seeds, blend the seeds with all the wet ingredients in a blender. If you don't like overly sweet treats, substitute coconut sugar for the regular sugar in the donuts. Skip the frosting or top the donuts with fresh strawberries. Alternatively, frost the donuts with Cashew Cream (page 144) flavored with freeze-dried strawberry powder or strawberry puree.

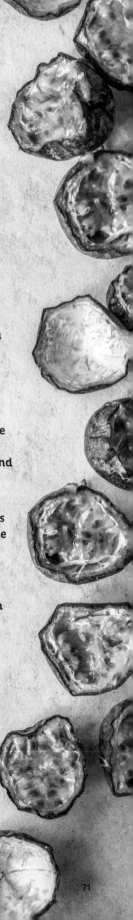

This is a tropical and fun recipe for when you're craving something comforting but refreshing! Interestingly, the viscous texture of the passionfruit puree acts as a binder instead of eggs. The bananas give the loaf extra moisture and sweetness. However, extra sugar is needed to balance out the tartness of the passionfruit. The high amount of fruit in this recipe makes a dense and moist loaf.

EASY BANANA AND PASSIONFRUIT BREAD

YIELD: 1 LOAF OR 8 SERVINGS

DRY INGREDIENTS

1½ cups (240 g) white rice flour or (188 g) all-purpose flour

1½ cups (168 g) almond meal

⅔ cup (96 g) coconut sugar

1 tablespoon (14 g) baking powder

WET INGREDIENTS

2 ripe bananas (about 8½ ounces, or 240 g)

3 passionfruit, puree only (about 4 ounces, or 110 g)

1¼ cup (285 ml) plant-based milk, such as almond, soy, or coconut

3 tablespoons (45 ml) sunflower or olive oil

DECORATIONSS

1 cup (170 g) plant-based yogurt, such as coconut, soy, or almond

Extra passionfruit puree, as desired

1} Preheat the oven to 325°F (160°C, or gas mark 3). Line a 9 × 4-inch (23 × 10 cm) loaf pan with parchment paper.

2} Add all the dry ingredients to a large bowl or food processor. Mix until there are no lumps and everything is combined.

3} In a separate bowl, mash the bananas and mix with the passionfruit, breaking up any long strands of puree. Add the fruit and the wet ingredients to the dry ingredients and mix until all the ingredients are evenly incorporated.

4} Pour the mixture into a loaf pan and bake for 1 hour or until a skewer can be inserted into the middle and there is no raw batter on it. The loaf will be slightly moist from the high amount of fruit. Let the loaf cool in the pan.

5} When the loaf is completely cool, spread with yogurt and passionfruit puree. Store it in an airtight container in the fridge for up to 5 days. The loaf can be kept at room temperature for a few days or in the freezer for up to 1 month without the yogurt frosting.

TIP

Substitutions: If you cannot eat almonds, you may substitute the almond meal with 1 cup (125 g) of all-purpose flour. However, this will result in a slightly chewy loaf due to the high amount of passionfruit.

This isn't really a quick recipe to make, but the dried pear slices are a convenient snack! I naturally colored the pears with superfood powders and a sprinkling of sugar, which gives the pears a beautiful shine. They are really eye-catching and can be used to decorate desserts, such as the Rainbow Pear Chai Cake on page 114. The color of the pears and superfood colors will change when dehydrated. Some of the colors may intensify or become darker while other colors will mix into nearby colors. The dehydrated pears are sweet and chewy like candy and may have a very subtle taste from the superfood powders.

DRIED RAINBOW PEAR SLICES

YIELD: 4 TO 8 SERVINGS

4 medium-size pears
(I used green Packham pears.)

8 teaspoons (32 g) light-colored granulated sugar

1 teaspoon pink pitaya or beetroot powder

1 teaspoon blue spirulina or butterfly pea flower powder

1 teaspoon matcha powder

1 teaspoon black goji powder

TIP

Feel free to use whatever superfood powders are available in your area! The more sugar you use, the shinier your pear slices will be.

1} Use a mandolin slicer or a sharp knife to cut the pears in ⅛-inch (3 mm) slices, lengthwise.

2} Divide the sugar between 4 bowls, placing 2 teaspoons of sugar in each bowl. Add 1 superfood powder to each bowl. Mix the ingredients in each bowl so the sugar is combined with the powder.

3} To make a pear slice one color, sprinkle 1 colored sugar over the whole slice and rub the sugar into the pear with your fingers, making sure it is covered. For a rainbow effect, sprinkle several colored sugars onto different sections of the pear slice and rub in the sugar. If desired, you can also color the other side of the pear, although this is not necessary if you're using the pears to decorate a cake as you will only see one side. Repeat the process for the remaining pear slices and colored sugar.

4} Place all the colored pears on a lined dehydrator tray or baking tray. The slices can be close to each other, but make sure they don't overlap.

5} Dehydrate the pear slices at 160°F (71°C) for 8 to 10 hours. Alternatively, bake the pear slices at your lowest oven temperature until the pears are dry when you squeeze them. If you are in a humid climate, you may have to dehydrate the pears for up to 12 hours. Store the pears in an airtight container in the fridge for up to 2 months.

One of my favorite things to do in my spare time is to catch up with friends in a cafe with a piece of cake (or a few), a cup of tea, and a good long chat!

—

The recipes in this chapter allow you to bring cafe-style treats to the comfort of your own home. I used to make several of these treats for cafes in my city and frequently received requests for the recipes. I'm excited to finally share these with you!

Cafe-Style
TREATS AT HOME

CLASSIC BUTTERY SCONES

YIELD: 20 MINI SCONES

1⅔ cups (200 g) self-rising flour

3 tablespoons (23 g) powdered sugar

1 teaspoon cream of tartar

½ teaspoon baking soda

¼ cup (55 g) vegan butter (if your butter isn't salted, add ½ teaspoon salt) + extra for brushing

½ cup + 1 tablespoon (135 ml) plant-based milk, such as almond, soy, or coconut

Raspberry Chia Jam (page 139) and Whipped Coconut Cream Frosting (page 148), to serve

1} Preheat the oven to 425°F (220°C, or gas mark 7) and lightly butter a baking tray.

2} Sift the flour, powdered sugar, cream of tartar, and baking soda into a bowl. Add the vegan butter and rub it in with your fingertips until there are no lumps of butter and the flour becomes large flaky crumbs. Add the milk to the bowl and stir with a butter knife until the mixture forms a soft dough.

3} Lightly dust a clean surface and place the dough on top. Use a rolling pin to gently roll the dough to ½ inch (1.3 cm) thick. Dust a circular cookie cutter in flour and press it into the dough to create scones. Arrange the scones in the baking tray so each one is touching each other. Brush the scones with extra vegan butter.

4} Bake the scones for 10 to 15 minutes, depending on the size of your scones. Enjoy immediately with Raspberry Chia Jam and Whipped Coconut Cream Frosting.

TIP

Use a baking tray with tall edges. Placing the scones right next to each other in the baking tray allows them to rise upwards (rather than sideways), which creates beautiful and cute scones!

These are classic shortbread cookies made with a more wholesome flour and without the processed margarine or butter! And these cookies still taste "buttery" and crumble in your mouth like traditional shortbread. Eat the cookies plain or make cookie sandwiches with them using Raspberry Chia Jam or anything else you desire. Chilling the cookie dough firms up the liquid oil and makes the dough easier to handle. These cookies are amazing with a cup of tea while chatting to a loved one!

SPELL SHORTBREAD COOKIES

YIELD: 8 TO 10 SHORTBREAD SANDWICHES

COOKIES

2 cups (240 g) plain spelt flour

½ cup (120 ml) light-tasting vegetable oil, such as sunflower, or refined coconut

¼ cup (30 g) powdered sugar

Pinch of salt

FILLING (OPTIONAL)

⅓ recipe Raspberry Chia Jam (page 139)

1} Add all the cookie ingredients to a bowl or food processor. Mix until evenly combined. The dough should be quite soft but pliable and can be pinched between two fingers without breaking. If your dough is too dry, add 1 tablespoon (15 ml) of oil at a time and mix until there are no crumbs. If your dough is too wet, add 1 tablespoon (about 8 g) of flour at a time and mix until there is no excess oil. Set aside in an airtight container in the fridge for at least 20 minutes.

2} When you are ready to bake the cookies, preheat the oven to 350°F (180°C, or gas mark 4).

3} Dust a clean surface with a few tablespoons (about 30 g) of flour. Place the chilled dough on top and use a rolling pin to roll the dough out to about ¼ inch (6 mm) thick.

4} Cut out cookies using a cookie cutter, as desired. Gather the excess dough, gently remix, and roll it out again. Repeat until all the dough has been used up. Arrange the cookies on a lined baking tray with a little space between each cookie. If you used liquid oil, it may be difficult to lift the cookies from the floured surface to the baking tray. If so, use a cake scraper to transfer the cookies to the tray.

5} Bake the cookies in the oven for 15 minutes or until the edges are golden brown. Let them cool completely in the tray. If you're making cookie sandwiches, spread the Raspberry Chia Jam on half of the cookies and place another cookie on top.

6} Without jam, the cookies can be kept in an airtight container at room temperature for 3 days, in the fridge for 1 week, or in the freezer for up to 1 month. With jam, the cookies can be kept in the fridge for 1 week or in the freezer for up to 1 month.

CARAMEL SLICE

—

YIELD: 18 SMALL SLICES

*Caramel slices are available in
bakeries across Australia, and they are often
sickly sweet. However, I love this version as the
caramel is naturally sweetened with whole dates
and balanced with earthy nut or seed butter.
The crunchy base contrasts with the smooth filling
and creamy chocolate. I added a little coconut cream
to the chocolate topping to make it easier to cut,
but not too much coconut cream so as to maintain
the "snap" reminiscent of the chocolate on
conventional caramel slices.*

BASE

1½ cups (218 g) almonds, or any other nut or seed

⅓ cup (53 g) pitted dates, soaked in water for at least 4 hours

½ teaspoon ground cinnamon (optional)

Pinch of salt

CARAMEL LAYER

1½ cups (240 g) pitted dates, soaked in water for at least 4 hours

½ cup (130 g) almond butter, or any other nut or seed butter

3 tablespoons (42 g) coconut oil

2 tablespoons (40 g) coconut nectar or maple syrup (optional)

1 teaspoon lucama powder (optional)

CHOCOLATE GANACHE TOPPING

1 recipe DIY Chocolate (page 140) or 1⅓ cups (250 g) store-bought vegan chocolate, melted

2 tablespoons (28 ml) coconut cream

DECORATIONS (OPTIONAL)

Chopped pistachios and rose petals or whatever you have in your pantry, as desired

1⟩ Line an 8-inch (20 cm) square cake pan with parchment paper.

2⟩ **To make the base:** Add the almonds to a food processor and process until it forms coarse crumbs. Drain the dates and add them to the food processor with the cinnamon (if using) and salt. Process the ingredients until they are well combined. Scoop the mixture into the cake pan and press down to create a firm and even base.

3⟩ **To make the caramel layer:** Drain the dates and reserve the soaking liquid. Add the drained dates and rest of the ingredients to a high-powered blender. Blend on medium to high for 3 to 5 minutes or until the mixture is very smooth and has no more chunks of nuts or dates. If the mixture is quite thick or the oils are separating from the solids, add some of the reserved date liquid and blend again. Pour the caramel mixture on the top of the base and smooth the surface with the back of a large spoon or a cake scraper.

4⟩ **To make the chocolate ganache:** Add all the ingredients to a mixing bowl. Blend with a stick blender for 1 minute or until all the ingredients are fully combined and there are no oil streaks on top. Pour onto the caramel layer and decorate if desired. Set aside in the fridge or freezer overnight.

5⟩ Run a sharp knife under hot water, dry it with a tea towel, and cut the slice straight from the freezer. The freezer firms up the caramel, preventing the chocolate from crumbling when you cut into it.

TIP

*The caramel in this slice will melt in
your mouth. If you would like a firmer
caramel or need it to survive at room
temperature for a few hours, add
a few more tablespoons
(42 to 55 g) of coconut oil.*

CHOCOLATE CUPCAKES WITH A RAINBOW CASHEW BUTTERCREAM

YIELD: 12 CUPCAKES

In my cake business, I often use this recipe when catering for kid parties, adults who don't like overly sweet desserts, or those with allergies. Gluten-free flour blends can be temperamental and result in gummy baked goods, so I always balance it out with white rice flour and, if suitable, cocoa powder. The careful blend of flours and coconut sugar makes a fluffy cupcake and melt-in-your-mouth crumb that makes it barely distinguishable from cupcakes with gluten. For coloring my desserts, I only ever use wholefoods such as vegetables, fruits, or superfood powders.

DRY INGREDIENTS FOR CUPCAKES

1 cup (160 g) white rice flour

¾ cup (108 g) coconut sugar

½ cup (40 g) cocoa powder or raw cacao powder

⅓ cup (45 g) gluten-free flour blend

1 tablespoon (14 g) gluten-free baking powder

WET INGREDIENTS FOR CUPCAKES

1½ cups (355 ml) plant-based milk, such as almond, soy, or coconut

½ cup (120 ml) light-tasting vegetable oil, such as sunflower

¼ cup (45 g) vegan chocolate, melted

RAINBOW CASHEW BUTTERCREAM

1 recipe Cashew Buttercream (page 147)

¼ cup raspberries, (31 g) fresh or (35 g) frozen + pinch of beetroot powder

¼ cup blueberries, (36 g) fresh or (39 g) frozen + pinch of beetroot powder

Handful of baby spinach and a few drops of peppermint extract

½ teaspoon blue spirulina

1} Preheat the oven to 350°F (180°C, or gas mark 4).

2} Add all the dry ingredients to a large bowl or food processor. Mix until there are no lumps and everything is combined. Add the wet ingredients and then mix thoroughly until the ingredients are evenly incorporated.

3} Scoop the batter into lined cupcake molds. Bake for 20 to 25 minutes or until a skewer can be inserted into a cupcake and it comes out clean. Place the cupcakes on a wire rack to cool.

4} **To make the rainbow cashew buttercream:** Divide the buttercream between 4 bowls. To make a pink buttercream, add the raspberries and beetroot powder to one bowl and blend with a stick blender. To make purple buttercream, add the blueberries and beetroot powder to another bowl and blend with a stick blender. Make green buttercream using spinach and blue using blue spirulina.

5} **To frost the cupcakes:** For an easier method, you can spread the frosting on the cupcakes with a spoon or butter knife. Alternatively, scoop the buttercream into a piping bag with a star nozzle and pipe as desired.

6} The cupcakes can be stored at room temperature for up to 2 to 4 hours, in an airtight container in the fridge for up to 3 days, or in the freezer for up to 1 month.

TIP

The cupcakes can be made nut-free by substituting soaked sunflower seeds for the soaked cashews in the Cashew Buttercream or by using the American-style Buttercream recipe on page 146.

If you can have gluten, use the recipe for the Customizable Baked Chocolate cake (page 117) instead and bake them in cupcake molds.

TIP
───

If you prefer fully raw cheesecakes, reduce your berries in a dehydrator. Dehydrate them at 115°F (46°C) for 6 to 8 hours or until they reach a jam-like consistency.

BERRY AND LEMON CHEESECAKES

YIELD: 8 INDIVIDUAL CHEESECAKES
WITH PIPING

Unbaked vegan cheesecakes mimic the taste and texture of conventional cheesecakes as the creamy filling is made by blending nuts and liquids in a high-powered blender. In these cheesecakes, the berries have a subtle natural sweetness that is brought out by the tartness of lemon. Plus, the berries impart a gorgeous color! I reduced the berries on the stovetop to bring out their subtle flavor and to evaporate any water (to prevent the cheesecakes from crystallizing if you store them in the freezer).

BASE

1 cup (145 g) almonds

⅓ cup (53 g) pitted dates, soaked in water for at least 2 hours

½ teaspoon ground cinnamon

Pinch of salt

CHEESECAKE LAYERS

1 cup (145 g) fresh or (155 g) frozen blueberries, (125 g) raspberries, or berries of choice

2½ cups (350 g) cashews, soaked in water for at least 4 hours

1 cup (235 ml) coconut cream, canned and only the thick white part at the top of the can

½ cup (112 g) coconut oil, melted

⅓ cup (80 ml) + 2 tablespoons (28 ml) melted cacao butter, divided

¼–½ cup (80–100 g) rice malt or maple syrup, or any other plant-based liquid sweetener to taste

Pinch of salt

2 tablespoons (28 ml) fresh lemon juice and the zest of those lemons

Dash of vanilla extract

Pinch of turmeric

1} **To make the base:** Process the almonds in a food processor until they form small crumbs. Drain the dates and add them to the food processor with the cinnamon and salt. Process until the mixture comes together. Press the mixture in the bases of cupcake silicon molds and set aside.

2} **To prepare the berry puree:** Add the berries to a small saucepan over medium-high heat. Boil while stirring for 5 minutes or until the berries break down and most of the berry juice evaporates. Set aside.

3} **To make the cheesecake filling:** Drain the cashews. Add them to a high-powered blender with the coconut cream, coconut oil, ⅓ cup (80 ml) of melted cacao butter, sweetener, and salt and blend until the mixture is smooth. Divide the mixture between 2 bowls. Add the lemon juice, lemon zest, vanilla, and turmeric to one bowl and mix. Spoon the lemon cheesecake into the cupcake molds, filling each halfway. Put the molds in the freezer and the remaining lemon cheesecake mixture in the fridge.

4} Add the berry puree and 2 tablespoons (28 ml) melted cacao butter to the remaining plain cheesecake mixture and puree with a stick blender or a stand blender until smooth. When the lemon cheesecake mixture in the molds is dry to the touch, fill the molds with the berry cheesecake. Return the molds to the freezer and put the remaining berry cheesecake in the fridge.

5} When the cheesecake surface is firm to the touch and the sides can be squeezed without resistance, carefully remove them from the silicone molds.

6} **To decorate:** When the leftover cheesecake mixture has firmed up, it can be used for piping. The mixture should be the consistency of thick buttercream. If it is too runny, let it set in the fridge for longer. If it is too firm, let it soften at room temperature. The mixture needs to be very smooth to be piped. Put the cheesecake mixture in a piping bag and decorate cupcakes as desired.

7} The cheesecakes can be stored in an airtight container in the fridge for up to 5 days or in the freezer for up to 1 month.

Anggur
manis
1 Kilo
rm
7.00

In Australia we refer to the wibbly-wobbly layer as jelly, but those of you from North America and Canada are probably used to seeing it called (vegan) gelatin. Whatever you call it though, it's delicious!

A fancy take on the classic peanut butter and jelly bar! The base is crunchy, the middle layer is creamy, and the jelly layer is bouncy gelatin! For the jelly, most recipes would ask you to remove the berry pulp, but to minimize food waste I kept the pulp in the jelly. Conventional gelatin is derived from animal bones, so I used agar powder, which is a seaweed extract. Agar can be found in Asian and health food stores.

ALMOND BUTTER AND BERRY "JELLY" BAR

———

YIELD: 16 SMALL SQUARE BARS

BASE

1 cup (145 g) almonds

1 cup (85 g) desiccated coconut

⅔ cup (107 g) pitted dates

Dash of ground cinnamon

ALMOND BUTTER LAYER

¾ cup (105 g) cashews, soaked in water for at least 4 hours

½ cup (130 g) almond butter

¾ cup (175 ml) canned coconut cream

2–4 tablespoons (40–80 g) rice malt or maple syrup, or any other plant-based liquid sweetener, to taste

¼ cup (55 g) cacao butter, melted

Pinch of salt

JELLY LAYER

1 cup (235 ml) water

1 cup (about 150 g) fresh or frozen berries of choice

3 tablespoons (60 g) rice malt or maple syrup, or any other plant-based liquid sweetener (optional)

1½ teaspoons agar powder

½ cup (65 g) fresh raspberries, sliced in half lengthways

1} Line an 8-inch (20 cm) square cake pan with parchment paper.

2} **To make the base:** Add the almonds and coconut to a food processor and process until it forms coarse crumbs. Drain the dates and add them to the food processor with the cinnamon. Process the ingredients until they are well combined. Scoop the mixture into the cake pan and press it down to create a firm and even base.

3} **To make the almond butter layer:** Drain the cashews and add them to a high-powered blender with the rest of the ingredients. Blend on medium to high for 3 to 5 minutes or until the mixture is very smooth. Pour the cheesecake mixture on the top of the base and smooth the surface with the back of a large spoon or a cake scraper. Place it in the freezer for at least 2 hours.

4} **To make the jelly layer:** When the almond butter layer is firm to the touch, add the water, 1 cup (about 150 g) of berries, sweetener (if using), and agar powder to a small saucepan. Blend with a stick blender until there are no more large chunks of berries. Bring the mixture to a gentle boil for 1 minute and then remove from the heat to cool slightly. Carefully pour the jelly on top of the almond butter layer and quickly arrange the sliced raspberries in the jelly. Place it in the fridge for 2 hours or until set.

5} Use a sharp knife to cut into bars. Enjoy immediately or store in an airtight container in the fridge for up to 3 to 5 days. The bars cannot be frozen as the jelly layer will crystallize.

TIP

———

Some agar fun facts:

Recipes with agar need to be boiled to activate the agar.

Jelly made with agar is stable at room temperature, unlike gelatin. This means no melting jelly, yay!

Agar gives jelly a "crisp" mouthfeel, and you have to try it for yourself to see if you'll like it. I personally love it!

TIP

If you don't have cacao butter, you can replace it with the same quantity of coconut oil.

COOKIE, CARAMEL, AND CHOCOLATE ICE CREAM BAR

YIELD: 16 BARS

My favorite chocolate bar before I was vegan was definitely Twix. I loved the contrast of crunchy shortbread with the sweet chewy caramel and how it's all encased in a brittle chocolate. I took these elements and combined it with ice cream to create a delectable treat perfect for the warmer months. I use coconut flour in the base as it's very absorbent, which allows the base to stay crunchy. However, I counteracted the dryness of coconut flour with almond meal, which has natural oils in it. For the ice cream layer, I use a combination of ingredients that don't completely solidify in the freezer, which means you won't break your teeth when devouring the bar!

BASE

1⅓ cups (149 g) almond meal

½ cup (56 g) coconut flour

⅓ cup (80 ml) light-tasting vegetable oil, such as sunflower

3 tablespoons (45 ml) aquafaba

2 tablespoons (40 g) rice malt or maple syrup, or any other plant-based liquid sweetener

CARAMEL ICE CREAM LAYER

1¼ (200 g) pitted dates, soaked in water for at least 4 hours

About 2 medium-size bananas (about 8½ ounces, or 240 g), peeled and frozen into chunks

½ cup (130 g) any nut or seed butter

COATING

1½ recipes DIY Chocolate (page 140) or 2 cups (375 g) store-bought vegan chocolate

1} Preheat the oven to 325°F (160°C, or gas mark 3). Line an 8-inch (20 cm) square baking pan with parchment paper.

2} **To make the base:** Add all the ingredients to a food processor or mixing bowl and mix until well combined. Press firmly into the baking pan, making sure there are no gaps. Smooth the surface with the back of a spoon, spatula, or cake scraper.

3} Bake in the oven for 10 to 12 minutes or until the edges are light golden brown. Leave the base in the pan to cool completely.

4} When the base has cooled, make the caramel ice cream layer: Add all the ingredients to a high-powered blender and blend until as smooth as possible. Scoop the ice cream on to the base and smooth the surface. Place it in the freezer for at least 4 hours or until the caramel is firm and dry to the touch.

5} **To make the coating:** Add the chocolate to a medium-size saucepan or a double boiler over low heat and melt.

6} Remove it from the freezer. Use a sharp knife to cut the bars as desired. When the bars are firm, carefully dip each one into the chocolate. Enjoy immediately or store the bars in the freezer for up to 2 months.

WHOLESOME WAGON WHEELS

YIELD: 16 SMALL SQUARE BARS

This is a more wholesome version of wagon wheels—a popular supermarket treat I loved as a kid! The trickiest—and most magical—thing in this recipe is the marshmallow, which is made without animal-derived gelatin and without refined sweeteners. I've written the recipe so the aquafaba has reached stiff peaks at the same time as when your syrup has been heated. The agar powder in the syrup sets quickly so it needs to be incorporated into the aquafaba and spread onto the base as quickly as possible. The marshmallow is only mildly sweet, which makes it perfect for adults!

SHORTBREAD BASE

1½ cups (188 g) all-purpose flour

⅓ cup (80 ml) light-tasting vegetable oil, such as sunflower

3 tablespoons (27 g) coconut sugar

2–4 tablespoons (28–60 ml) water

Pinch of salt

RASPBERRY CHIA JAM

1 recipe Raspberry Chia Jam (page 139) or ¾ cup (about 240 g) store-bought raspberry jam

MARSHMALLOW LAYER

⅓ cup (80 ml) aquafaba

¼ tsp cream of tartar

¼ cup (80 g) rice malt syrup

¼ cup (60 g) water

1 tablespoon (9 g) agar powder

Dash of vanilla extract or vanilla bean powder

CHOCOLATE LAYER

1 recipe DIY Chocolate (page 140) or 1⅓ cups (250 g) store-bought vegan chocolate

2 tablespoons (28 ml) coconut cream

TIP

For a gluten-free base, use the short crust pastry recipe for the Fig and Pear Tart (page 99), but use only ¾ of the quantity of ingredients.

1} Preheat the oven to 350°F (180°C, or gas mark 4). Line an 8-inch (20 cm) square baking pan with parchment paper.

2} **To make the shortbread base:** Combine all the ingredients in a medium-size bowl. If the mixture is crumbly, add extra water and mix until it becomes a pliable dough. Firmly press the mixture into the baking pan and smooth the surface. Bake for 20 to 25 minutes or until the surface is light brown. Allow the base to cool in the baking pan.

3} When the base has cooled, spread the Raspberry Chia Jam evenly on top. Set aside in the fridge.

4} **To make the marshmallow layer:** Add the aquafaba and cream of tartar to a stand mixer or large mixing bowl. Start to whip on high speed. Meanwhile, mix the syrup, water, agar, and vanilla in a small saucepan and place it over high heat. Once the mixture starts to boil, remove the saucepan from the heat. When the aquafaba has formed stiff peaks, slowly pour the hot syrup into the aquafaba while whipping at the same time. The mixture may deflate or separate for a few seconds; this is normal. Continue whipping and scrape down the sides of the bowl until all the ingredients are well combined. When the mixture is thick and glossy, quickly spread the marshmallow onto the base and smooth the surface. Put the pan in the fridge to set for at least 2 hours.

5} When the marshmallow is firm to the touch, gently melt the chocolate and coconut cream in a small saucepan. Pour the chocolate over the marshmallow layer and return it to the fridge to set.

6} **To slice:** Run a sharp knife under hot water and dry with a tea towel. Use the warm knife to gently cut through the chocolate layer and the remainder of the bar. Eat immediately or store in an airtight container in the fridge for up to 1 week. These bars will not freeze.

FIG AND PEAR TART WITH A CARDAMOM COCONUT CREAM

YIELD: 8 SERVINGS

Here's a wholesome tart for more sophisticated palettes! This tart is naturally sweetened with dried figs, pears, and just a little coconut sugar. I enhanced the fruits' natural sweetness by boiling the figs into a jam and roasting the pears. The spices add depth and warmth, making this tart a really comforting dessert. The tart base is gluten-free and has a delicate crumb thanks to the almond meal, but it is not too crumbly as the tapioca starch binds the ingredients together.

BASE

¾ cup (120 g) white rice flour

¾ cup (84 g) almond meal

½ cup (60 g) tapioca starch

½ cup (120 ml) light-tasting vegetable oil, such as sunflower

⅓ cup (80 ml) water

3 tablespoons (27 g) coconut sugar

Pinch of salt

FILLING

1 cup (150 g) packed dried figs, stems removed

¾ cup (175 ml) water

1 teaspoon ground cinnamon

½ teaspoon ground ginger

½ teaspoon ground nutmeg

3 medium-size pears

CARDAMOM COCONUT CREAM

½ recipe Whipped Coconut Cream Frosting (page 148)

1 teaspoon ground cardamom

TIP

If you can have gluten, you can use the following ingredients for the short crust pastry: 1½ cups (188 g) all-purpose flour, ⅓ cup (80 ml) light-tasting vegetable oil, such as sunflower, and 3 tablespoons (27 g) coconut sugar. Add a tablespoon (15 ml) of water at a time if the dough is too dry.

1} Preheat the oven to 325°F (160°C, or gas mark 3). Line or grease an 8½-inch (22 cm) loose bottom or springform tart pan.

2} **To make the base:** Add all the ingredients to a mixing bowl or food processor and mix until evenly combined and it forms a dough. The dough should be soft but pliable and can be pinched between two fingers without breaking. Add the dough directly to the tart pan and press it against the bottom and sides to form a crust. Make sure there are no holes and the crust is as even as possible. Set aside in the fridge.

3} **To make the filling:** Roughly chop the figs and add them to a small saucepan with the water and spices. Bring to a boil for 5 minutes and then reduce to a medium-low heat and simmer while stirring occasionally. After 5 to 10 minutes or when the figs easily break apart, remove the saucepan from the heat. Puree the figs with a stick blender until they turn into a thick jam-like consistency.

4} Remove the cores from the pears, halve the pears, and then thinly slice. Make sure the slices are about the same thickness to ensure they cook at the same rate.

5} **To assemble:** Spread ¾ of the fig jam on the base and sides of the crust. Arrange the pear slices on top as desired, alternating with the remaining fig jam. The jam in between the pear slices allows the pears to remain in place.

6} Bake for 30 minutes or until the pear slices have softened. Test this by poking a knife in a pear slice in the middle of the tart. Cool for 5 minutes in the tart pan and carefully remove onto a serving plate.

7} **To make the cardamom coconut cream:** Follow the instructions on page 148 to make the Whipped Coconut Cream Frosting. Gently mix the cardamom into the cream.

8} Serve the tart warm with the Cardomom Coconut Cream. Store the tart in airtight container in the fridge for up to 5 days.

BAKLAVA CUSTARD TART

YIELD: 8 SERVINGS

BAKLAVA FILLING AND TOPPING

¾ cup (75 g) walnuts

½ cup (62 g) pistachios

¼ cup (80 g) maple syrup

1 teaspoon ground cinnamon

Few drops of rose water (optional)

Few drops of lemon juice (optional)

BASE

8 sheets of filo pastry, defrosted according to packet instructions

¼ cup (60 ml) light-tasting vegetable oil, such as sunflower

CUSTARD LAYER

½ cup (55 g) cornstarch

2½ cups (570 ml) soymilk

¼ cup (80 g) maple syrup, to taste, plus more for drizzling

1 tablespoon (9 g) agar powder

2 teaspoons vanilla extract

Pinch of salt

Pinch of turmeric powder, to color

TIP

Don't worry if your filo pastry breaks. When you layer all your filo pastry, you won't notice! After you pour the custard into the tart, make sure the tart doesn't change temperature dramatically; otherwise, the custard will crack.

I don't often like to choose favorites, but if I HAD to pick my favorite recipes from this cookbook, this baklava custard tart would be up there! Just like conventional baklava, this tart has loads of nuts, crispy filo pastry, and multiple layers. I took it to another level by combining it with my favorite childhood treat, custard! Instead of thickening the custard with eggs, I used cornstarch, which is much easier to use! The subtle vanilla and sweetness from the custard perfectly complements a punchy and flavorsome baklava filling.

1} Preheat the oven to 350°F (180°C, or gas mark 4). Add the walnuts and pistachios to a food processor. Pulse until it reaches coarse crumbs, and then remove the blade of the food processor. Add the maple syrup, cinnamon, and rose water (if using) to the nuts and mix with a spoon. Set aside.

2} **To make the base:** Line a tart pan with parchment paper. If your filo pastry is rectangular, cut it in half along the width. Place one layer of filo pastry in the tart pan, allowing the ends of the pastry to protrude from the pan. Brush the pastry with oil and repeat with half of the pastry to cover the entire tart pan. Scoop a few tablespoons (45 to 55 g) of the baklava mixture on the base of the tart and spread it evenly. Layer and repeat with the remaining pastry. Bake the pastry in the oven for 10 to 15 minutes or until the middle of the tart is golden.

3} **To make the custard:** Add the cornstarch to a medium-size, deep saucepan with just enough soymilk to cover. Whisk until there are no more lumps of cornstarch. Add all the remaining custard ingredients to the saucepan and place it over high heat. Bring the custard to a boil for 3 minutes while whisking to make sure it doesn't stick to the bottom of the pan. Reduce to medium-low heat and whisk for around 10 minutes or until it reaches a thick custard consistency. If there are lumps in your custard, blend it with a stick blender until it is smooth. Set aside the saucepan to cool for about 15 minutes.

4} **To assemble:** While the custard is warm (but not hot), slowly pour it into your tart base. If needed, smooth the surface with the back of a spoon. Leave the tart at room temperature for about 30 minutes and then set aside in the fridge for at least 2 hours or overnight.

5} **To serve:** When the custard has fully set, sprinkle with the remaining baklava topping and drizzle with additional maple syrup.

VERY BERRY PIE INFUSED WITH CHAMOMILE

YIELD: 8 TO 12 SERVINGS

This pie is as easy or complicated as you make it! For a quick pie, you can just purchase plant-based pastry and fill it with this recipe's berry filling. For a simple pie, you can make a plain pastry and top the pie with just one piece of pastry. For a more complicated pie, you can flavor and color the pastry with raspberries, infuse the filling with tea, and create a fancy design on top. It's basically a "choose your own adventure" pie!

BERRY FILLING

¼ cup (80 g) rice malt or maple syrup, or any other plant-based liquid sweetener to taste

2 teaspoons or 2 teabags of chamomile tea or tea of choice (optional)

¼ cup (30 g) cornstarch

1 teaspoon ground cinnamon (optional)

2 cups blueberries, (290 g) fresh or (310 g) frozen

PASTRY

1 cup raspberries, (125 g) fresh or (140 g) frozen (optional)

1 cup (125 g) all-purpose flour + more for rolling

½ cup (120 ml) light-tasting oil, such as sunflower or refined coconut, or (112 g) vegan butter

¼ cup (48 g) white vegan sugar or (36 g) coconut sugar

2 tablespoons (28 ml) water

1 tablespoon (10 g) beetroot powder (optional)

TIPS

When the pie is baked, the pastry will turn a rustic pink-brown color.

For a gluten-free base, use the short crust pastry recipe for the Fig and Pear Tart (page 99), but use ¾ of the quantity of ingredients.

1} For the berry filling, add the liquid sweetener and a splash of water to a small saucepan. Bring to a boil and then remove from the heat. Steep the tea leaves or bags (if using) in sweetener and set aside.

2} **To make the pastry:** Add the raspberries (if using) to a small saucepan with a splash of water over medium heat. Simmer until the raspberries have broken down and most of the juice has evaporated. Set aside the raspberries to cool.

3} When the raspberries have cooled to room temperature, blend them with a stick blender until smooth. Combine the pureé and all the pastry ingredients in a food processor or a large mixing bowl. Process or mix until just combined and the pastry forms a pliable ball. Divide the mixture into 2 balls and set 1 aside in an airtight container in the fridge.

4} Dust a clean surface with all-purpose flour. Use a rolling pin to flatten the pastry into a circle slightly bigger than your pie pan; I used an 8-inch (20 cm) pie pan and rolled the pastry about ¼ inch (6 mm) thick. Wrap the pastry around the rolling pin and carefully unwrap the pastry over the pie pan. Press the pastry against the pan to form a crust and cut off any excess. If your pastry breaks, simply patch it up with more pastry.

5} **To make the berry filling:** Remove the tea leaves or bags from the sweetner. Add the sweetener, cornstarch, cinnamon (if using), and blueberries to a large bowl and toss until the blueberries are covered in syrup. Fill the pie crust with the blueberries.

6} Roll out the remaining pastry and decorate your pie as desired.

7} Bake in the oven for 30 to 40 minutes or until a knife or skewer can be inserted into the middle and the base feels firm. Remove from the oven and let the pie cool in the pan on a wire rack. The blueberry filling will thicken as the pie cools. Enjoy the pie warm or store in an airtight container in the fridge to enjoy later.

UNBAKED NOTELLA CHEESECAKE

YIELD: 12 SERVINGS

My favorite unbaked treat is definitely this notella cheesecake! It mimics the taste of a popular hazelnut chocolate spread just with roast hazelnuts, cacao powder, and a sweetener. The crunchy nuts in the base complement the smooth cheesecake. I added a layer of vanilla cheesecake to balance out the richness of the notella layer.

BASE

1 cup (135 g) roasted hazelnuts

1 cup (145 g) almonds, (100 g) pecans, or (100 g) walnuts

¾ cup (120 g) pitted dates, soaked in water for at least 4 hours

¼ cup (20 g) raw cacao or cocoa powder

Pinch of salt

NOTELLA CHEESECAKE LAYER

¾ cup (105 g) cashews, soaked in water for at least 4 hours

¾ cup (101 g) roasted hazelnuts

¾ cup (175 ml) canned coconut cream

⅓ cup (107 g) rice malt or maple syrup, or any other plant-based liquid sweetener

¼ cup (60 ml) melted cacao butter

VANILLA CHEESECAKE LAYER

1⅔ cup (233 g) cashews, soaked in water for at least 4 hours

¾ cup (175 ml) canned coconut cream

⅓ cup (80 ml) melted coconut oil

3 tablespoons (45 ml) melted cacao butter

2 tablespoons (40 g) rice malt or maple syrup, or any other plant-based liquid sweetener

1 teaspoon vanilla extract or vanilla bean powder

Pinch of salt

DECORATIONS (OPTIONAL)

1 recipe Raspberry Chia Jam (page 139)

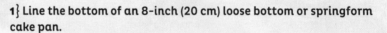

1} Line the bottom of an 8-inch (20 cm) loose bottom or springform cake pan.

2} **To make the base:** Add the nuts to a food processor and process until it forms coarse crumbs. Drain the dates and add them to the food processor with the cacao powder and salt. Process until they are well combined. Scoop the mixture into the cake pan and press it down to create a firm and even base.

3} **To make the vanilla cheesecake:** Drain the cashews and add them to a high-powered blender with the rest of the layer ingredients. Blend on medium to high for 3 to 5 minutes or until the mixture is very smooth. Pour the cheesecake mixture on the top of the base and smooth the surface with the back of a large spoon or a cake scraper. Set aside the cake in the freezer for at least 2 hours.

4} **To make the notella cheesecake:** Repeat the method for the vanilla cheesecake but using the ingredients listed under the notella cheesecake layer. If desired, reserve some of the notella cheesecake for decorating the cake. When the vanilla layer is dry to the touch, pour the notella cheesecake on top. Set the cake aside in the freezer or fridge for about 4 hours or until it is firm to the touch. Remove the cake from the cake pan, decorate as desired, and slice with a sharp knife. Serve the cake immediately or store it in an airtight container in the fridge for up to 5 days or in the freezer for up to 1 month.

TIP

The cake will keep at room temperature for up to 1 hour if it is around 65°F or 18°C. If you would like to keep the cake for any longer at room temperature, I recommend that you freeze the cake beforehand to ensure the cake lasts longer or to keep it with ice packs in a portable cooler.

POMEGRANATE YOGURT CAKE

YIELD: 8 TO 10 SERVINGS

The beautiful pink pomegranate glaze makes this cake a showstopper at any celebration! It's infused with exotic spices and pistachios, which makes it perfect with a cup of tea! Plant-based yogurt makes the cake extra moist, and its acidity balances out with the sweetness. The yogurt makes the cake denser than classic sponge cakes but baking the cake in a Bundt pan helps the cake cook more evenly. Of course, you can use a normal circular cake pan but make sure you use a wide 10-inch (25 cm) pan to ensure the middle of the cake bakes.

CAKE

2 cups (240 g) self-rising flour

1 cup (200 g) granulated sugar or (144 g) coconut sugar, to taste

1 teaspoon baking powder

½ cup (62 g) raw pistachios, ground into fine crumbs (optional)

2 teaspoons ground cinnamon

½ teaspoon ground cardamom

1½ cups (255 g) plant-based yogurt, such as coconut, soy, or almond

⅓ cup (80 ml) light-tasting vegetable oil, such as sunflower

¾ cup (175 ml) plant-based milk, such as almond, soy, or coconut

Dash of rose water (optional)

Zest of 1 orange or lemon (optional)

GLAZE (OPTIONAL)

1 cup (120 g) powdered sugar

Splash of plant-based milk, such as almond, soy, or coconut

Pinch of beetroot powder

DECORATIONS (OPTIONAL)

½ cup (87 g) pomegranate arils

¼ cup (31 g) raw pistachios, roughly chopped

1⟩ Preheat the oven to 325°F (170°C, or gas mark 3). Grease a 9-inch (22 cm) Bundt pan.

2⟩ **To make the cake:** Add all the flour, sugar, baking powder, pistachios (if using), and spices to a large bowl. Mix until combined and there are no lumps. Add the remaining cake ingredients and mix until combined. Pour the batter into the Bundt pan and bake for 55 minutes or until a skewer can be inserted into the cake and it comes out clean.

3⟩ Allow the cake to cool in the pan and then turn out onto a serving plate.

4⟩ **To make the glaze:** Add all the ingredients to a medium-size bowl and mix until smooth. Drizzle the glaze onto the cake and decorate it with pomegranate and pistachios as desired.

5⟩ Serve and enjoy. Store the cake in an airtight container in the fridge for 3 to 5 days or in the freezer for up to 1 month.

Dessert is better—and more delicious—
when it's shared with loved ones. You could be
celebrating the everyday or a special occasion!
These desserts are a bit more special, and
they have the wow factor so you can bring them
over to a friend's place. Of course, you're more
than welcome to enjoy these treats by yourself
because that's "self-care" right?!

Let's Share
AND CELEBRATE!

CUSTOMIZABLE CLASSIC BAKED VANILLA CAKE

YIELD: 8 TO 10 SERVINGS

This cake is fluffy, moist, and has a delicate crumb. I use this recipe as a foundation for all of my baked cake recipes so it's very customizable! When you make layered cakes, each layer needs to be as flat as possible. To achieve this, I set the oven temperature relatively low. I multiplied this recipe by 1½ for a three-layered cake (pictured) and paired it with the classic American-style Buttercream (page 146). For a single layered cake, use an 8-inch (20 cm) cake pan and bake it for more than 50 minutes.

DRY INGREDIENTS
2½ cups (300 g) self-rising flour

1½ cups (300 g) granulated sugar

1½ teaspoons baking powder

WET INGREDIENTS
2 cups (475 ml) plant-based milk, such as almond, soy, or coconut

⅔ cup (160 ml) light-tasting vegetable oil, such as sunflower

1 tablespoon (15 ml) apple cider vinegar or regular vinegar

1 teaspoon vanilla bean extract or powder

FROSTING
Your choice of frosting (pages 146–148)

HOW TO CUSTOMIZE

For a refined sugar-free cake, substitute the sugar with coconut sugar. Note that this will make the cake a light brown color.

For a less sweet cake, decrease the sugar to 1 cup (200 g). This amount of sugar is needed for the cake to maintain its structure. The less sugar you use, the denser the cake.

For a gluten-free cake, substitute the self-rising flour with ¾ cup (120 g) white rice flour and ½ cup (68 g) gluten-free flour blend, increase the baking powder to 4 teaspoons (18 g), and add a pinch of salt.

1} Preheat the oven to 325°F (160°C, or gas mark 3). Line two 6-inch (15 cm) cake pans with parchment paper or brush with oil.

2} **To make the cake:** In a large bowl, food processor, or stand mixer, whisk all the dry ingredients until combined and there are no lumps. Add all the cake wet ingredients and whisk until thoroughly combined and there are no lumps.

3} Evenly divide the cake batter into the 2 baking pans. Bake for 50 minutes or until a skewer can be inserted into the middle of each cake and it comes out clean. Let the cakes cool in the cake pans for about 30 minutes to 1 hour. Carefully remove the cakes from the pans and place them on a wire rack. Set aside the cakes in an airtight container in the fridge or freezer until you are ready to frost them (this helps minimize any breakage).

4} Prepare your desired frosting according to the instructions.

5} **To assemble the cake:** Using a serrated knife, slice the domes off the cakes, ensuring each is as flat as possible (save the scraps to enjoy later). Place one cake layer on a serving plate and generously spread a layer of frosting on the top. Gently place the next cake layer on the frosting making sure it is level. Spread a thin layer of icing on the sides and top of the cake and use a cake scraper to level it out. If desired, use the remaining frosting to decorate the top of the cake.

6} Serve immediately or set aside in the fridge in a large airtight container until ready to serve! Store the cake in the fridge for up to 5 days or in the freezer for up to 1 month.

This is a beautiful way to dress up a vanilla cake and to use up the Dried Rainbow Pear Slices (page 72)! Arranging the pears on the cake is a little fiddly, so make sure you are not in a rush. The result is well worth it, and the cake is a showstopper at any event. I once sold slices of this cake at a local vegan festival, and the slices attracted a lot of attention—and disappeared quickly. This recipe is great because there's cake for those who love fluffy baked treats AND dried pears, which are like pseudo-candy and are adored by kids!

RAINBOW PEAR CHAI CAKE

—

YIELD: 8 TO 12 SERVINGS

DECORATIONS

1 recipe of Dried Rainbow Pear Slices (page 72)

1 recipe American-style Buttercream (page 146) or Cashew Buttercream (page 147)

CAKE

1 recipe Customizable Classic Baked Vanilla Cake (page 113)

2 teaspoons chai spice

1} Prepare the pear slices at least 1 day beforehand.

2} **To make the cake:** Prepare the cake according to instructions, adding the chai spices to the dry ingredients. Frost the cake according to the instructions.

3} **To arrange the cake:** Stick the pears on the outside of the cake. Start by creating a row of pears at the bottom going toward the top of the cake. Allow some of the pears to hang off the top edges of the cake. Use extra frosting to stick the pears on the cake, if necessary.

4} **To serve:** Use a pair of scissors to cut through the pears on the outside and cut the cake as normal. Store the cake in an airtight container in the fridge for up to 5 days or in the freezer up to 1 month.

I might be biased but this is the best vegan chocolate cake I've ever eaten! It also happens to be the most requested cake in my business. It's moist, rich, and just melts in your mouth! You only need a few simple ingredients that you will probably already have in your pantry. I used two quantities of thick chocolate ganache to decorate this cake. For a single layered cake, use a 10-inch (25 cm) cake pan and bake for longer than 40 minutes.

CUSTOMIZABLE BAKED CHOCOLATE CAKE

YIELD: 8 TO 10 SERVINGS

DRY INGREDIENTS
2 cups (240 g) self-rising flour

1⅓ cup (267 g) granulated sugar

½ cup (40 g) cocoa powder

1½ teaspoons baking powder

WET INGREDIENTS
2 cups (475 ml) plant-based milk, such as almond, soy, or coconut

½ cup (120 ml) light-tasting vegetable oil, such as sunflower

¼ cup (55 g) melted vegan chocolate

FROSTING
Your choice of frosting (pages 146–148)

1} **Preheat the oven to 325°F (160°C, or gas mark 3). Line two 8-inch (20 cm) cake pans with parchment paper or brush with oil.**

2} **To make the cake: In a large bowl, food processor, or stand mixer, whisk all the dry ingredients until combined and there are no lumps. Add all the wet ingredients and whisk until thoroughly combined and there are no lumps.**

3} **Evenly divide the cake batter into the 2 baking pans. Bake for 35 to 40 minutes or until a skewer can be inserted into the middle of each cake and it comes out clean. Let the cakes cool in the cake pans for about 30 minutes to 1 hour. Carefully remove the cakes from the pans and place them on a wire rack. Set the cakes aside in an airtight container in the fridge or freezer until you are ready to frost them (this helps minimize any breakage).**

4} **To assemble the cake: If your cakes have domes, use a serrated knife to slice the domes off the cakes (save the scraps to enjoy later). Place one cake layer on a plate and generously spread frosting on the top. Gently place another cake layer on top. Spread additional frosting on the cake and decorate as desired.**

5} **Serve immediately or set aside in the fridge in a large airtight container until ready to serve. Store the cake in the fridge for up to 5 days or in the freezer for up to 1 month.**

HOW TO CUSTOMIZE

For a refined sugar-free, substitute the granulated sugar with coconut sugar.

For a less sweet cake cake, you can decrease the sugar to 1 cup (200 g). This amount of sugar is needed to maintain the structure of the cake. The less sugar you use, the denser the cake.

For a gluten-free cake, use the recipe for the Chocolate Cupcakes on page 84 and bake the recipe in 1 or 2 cake pans.

This shows you how easy it is to customize the chocolate cake on page 117! I transformed the cake into a classic alcohol-free Black Forest by adding cherries, which helps balance out the richness of the chocolate. The Black Forest is normally adorned with white frosting, which beautifully contrasts with the dark tones of the chocolate cake.

BLACK FOREST CAKE

YIELD: 14 TO 16 SERVINGS

CAKE

1½ recipes Customizable Baked Chocolate Cake (page 117)

DECORATION

1½ recipes American-style Buttercream (page 146), 1 recipe Cashew Buttercream (page 147) or 2 recipes Whipped Coconut Cream Frosting (page 148)

1 cup (155 g) fresh cherries

Powdered sugar, to serve (optional)

CHERRY COMPOTE

2 cups (310 g) frozen or fresh pitted cherries

1–2 tablespoons (15–28 ml) lemon juice, to taste

1–2 tablespoons (20–40 g) rice malt or maple syrup, or any other plant-based liquid sweetener

1 tablespoon (8 g) cornstarch

1} Prepare the chocolate cake according to instructions but bake it in three 8-inch (20 cm) cake pans.

2} Prepare the frosting according to instructions.

3} **To make the cherry compote:** Add the cherries, lemon juice, and liquid sweetener to a small saucepan over high heat. Boil for 5 to 10 minutes, smashing the cherries with the back of a fork. On the side, mix the cornstarch with a splash of water to make a slurry. Add the cornstarch mixture to the saucepan and stir to combine. The compote is ready when it has thickened to a jam-like consistency. Use a stick blender to blend half of the compote, leaving the other half lumpy. Set aside to cool.

4} **To assemble the cake:** If your cakes have domes, use a serrated knife to slice the domes off the cakes (save the scraps to enjoy later). Place one layer on a plate, spread ⅓ of the cherry compote on the cake and ⅓ of the frosting. Gently place another cake layer on top and repeat with the compote, frosting, and the remaining layer. Scatter the fresh cherries on top of the cake.

5} Serve immediately or set aside in the fridge in a large airtight container until ready to serve. If desired, dust with powdered sugar just before serving. Store the cake in the fridge for up to 5 days or in the freezer without the fresh cherries for up to 1 month.

BERRY CHOCOLATE MOUSSE TART

YIELD: 8 SERVINGS

If I had to make only one dessert for a dinner party to wow any guest, it would be this chocolate mousse tart! This is one of my most popular recipes on my website because it's so ridiculously delicious. The tart has a rich brownie crust that is covered with a layer of Raspberry Chia Jam, a decadent layer of chocolate mousse, and is topped with fresh berries! I've given this tart to tofu-haters, friends, and customers and they couldn't guess there was tofu in it! The cacao powder, chocolate, and unrefined sweetener helps mask the taste of the tofu.

BROWNIE CHOCOLATE BASE

2 cups (200 g) pecans

¼ cup (65 g) nut butter (almond, peanut, or any other nut butter would work)

½ cup (40 g) raw cacao or cocoa powder

12 pitted Medjool dates

Pinch of salt

RASPBERRY CHIA JAM

⅔ cup (93 g) frozen raspberries, defrosted

2 tablespoons (26 g) chia seeds

2 tablespoons (40 g) rice malt or maple syrup, or any other plant-based liquid sweetener

CHOCOLATE MOUSSE FILLING

1 cup (180 g) roughly chopped vegan chocolate

2 cups (500 g) silken soft tofu

½ cup (120 ml) canned coconut cream

½ cup (160 g) maple syrup, or any other plant-based liquid sweetener

½–¾ cup (40–60 g) raw cacao or cocoa powder, to taste

½ teaspoon vanilla bean powder

DECORATION

1 cup (about 150 g) fresh berries, such as blueberries and raspberries

1⟩ **To make the base:** Add the pecans to a food processor and process until it forms coarse crumbs. Add the remaining base ingredients and process until it stays together when it is pinched. Press the mixture into a lined tart pan. I used an 8-inch wide and 1½-inch deep (20 cm wide and 4 cm deep) tart pan. If you don't have a pan that deep, use a slightly bigger tin.

2⟩ **To make the raspberry chia jam:** Add all the ingredients to a small bowl and mash them with the back of a fork until the raspberries have broken down. Mix until combined and then set aside to thicken.

3⟩ **To make the filling:** Add the chocolate to a small saucepan or a double boiler over low heat and melt. Add all the filling ingredients to a food processor and process until as smooth as possible.

4⟩ **To assemble:** Spread the Raspberry Chia Jam along the bottom and sides of the tart base. Pour the chocolate mousse over the jam and smooth the top. Decorate with berries and whatever else you might like. Set aside the tart in the fridge for 4 hours or until set.

5⟩ Store the tart in the fridge for 3 to 5 days or in the freezer without the fresh berries for up to 1 month.

TIP

To make this tart nut-free, substitute sunflower seeds for the nuts in the base.

To make this tart soy-free, substitute the filling with the thin Chocolate Ganache (page 143).

SUMMERY FRUIT TART, TWO WAYS!

YIELD: 8 TO 10 SERVINGS

This creamy tart is perfect for gatherings in the warmer months! The first version of this tart is better for those who prefer more traditional desserts as it is baked and has a classic, crumbly base. The second version is better for those who are health-conscious as it is packed with nutritious nuts. Feel free to mix and match the bases and fillings!

OPTION 1: TART BASE

1½ cups (188 g) all-purpose flour

⅓ cup (80 ml) light-tasting vegetable oil, such as sunflower

3 tablespoons (27 g) coconut sugar

2–4 tablespoons (28–60 ml) water

OPTION 1: FILLING

1 heaped cup (140 g) cashews, soaked in water for at least 2 hours

¾ cup (188 g) silken firm tofu

¼ cup (60 ml) plant-based milk, such as almond, soy, or coconut

¼–½ cup (80–100 g) rice malt or maple syrup, or any other plant-based liquid sweetener to taste

½ cup (85 g) unsweetened plant-based yogurt (optional)

1 tablespoon (15 ml) vanilla extract

Zest and juice of ½ lemon

Pinch of salt

OPTION 2: TART BASE

1½ cups (218 g) almonds, or any other nut or seed

⅓ cup (53 g) pitted dates, soaked in water for at least 4 hours

Pinch of salt

OPTION 2: FILLING

1 cup (140 g) cashews, soaked in water for at least 4 hours

1 cup (235 ml) coconut cream

¼–½ cup (80–100 g) rice malt or maple syrup, or any other plant-based liquid sweetener to taste

3 tablespoons (42 g) cacao butter or coconut oil, melted

DECORATIONS

Mangoes, nectarines, passionfruit, or any other fruit in season!

OPTION 1

1} Preheat the oven to 325°F (160°C, or gas mark 3). Line the bottom of an 8-inch (20 cm) loose bottom tart pan.

2} **To make the tart base:** Combine all the ingredients in a medium-size bowl. If the mixture is crumbly, add extra water and mix until it becomes a pliable dough. Firmly press the mixture into the baking pan and smooth the surface. Set aside.

3} **To make the filling:** Add all the ingredients to a high-powered blender, blend until smooth, and then pour the mixture into the tart pan. Bake for 30 to 40 minutes or until the middle of the tart is not wobbly. Leave the tart in the oven with the door ajar. When the tart is cool, set it aside in the fridge to set further.

4} Slice the fruit and decorate the tart as desired. Serve immediately or set aside in the fridge in a large airtight container until ready to serve! Store in the fridge for up to 5 days.

OPTION 2

1} Line the bottom of an 8-inch (20 cm) loose bottom tart pan.

2} **To make the tart base:** Add the almonds to a food processor and process until it forms coarse crumbs. Drain the dates and add them to the food processor with the salt. Process until it is combined and stays together when it is pinched. Press the mixture into the tart pan.

3} **To make the filling:** Drain the cashews and add all the ingredients to a high-powered blender. Blend until it is as smooth as possible. Pour the mixture into the tart base. Set aside in the fridge to set for around 4 hours or until the cream is not wobbly in the middle.

4} Slice the fruit and decorate the tart as desired. Serve immediately or set aside in the fridge in a large airtight container until ready to serve! Store in the fridge for up to 5 days or in the freezer for up to 1 month.

EPIC PEANUT BUTTER–CHOCOLATE CAKE

YIELD: 12 TO 16 SERVINGS

Chocolate, peanut butter, and caramel is one of the best combinations! This cake has sooo many delicious layers and components that each one can be a dessert on its own. The base can be rolled into Snickers-inspired Bliss Balls; the cheesecake is a classic, creamy, peanut butter cheesecake; the next layer is essentially a caramel bar studded with peanuts; and it's all topped with a chocolate ganache and peanut brittle. When you combine the layers, it makes a taste explosion!

BASE

1 cup (145 g) roasted or raw peanuts

1 cup (145 g) sunflower seeds

¾ cup (120 g) pitted dates, soaked in water for at least 4 hours

¼ cup (20 g) raw cocoa or cacao powder

Pinch of salt

PEANUT BUTTER–CHEESECAKE LAYER

1 cup (140 g) cashews, soaked in water for at least 4 hours

¾ cup (175 ml) canned coconut cream

⅓ cup (80 ml) melted coconut oil

¼ cup (65 g) chunky or smooth peanut butter

3 tablespoons (45 ml) melted cacao butter

2 tablespoons (40 g) rice malt or maple syrup, or any other plant-based liquid sweetener

PEANUT BUTTER–CARAMEL LAYER

1 cup (145 g) peanuts

1 cup (140 g) cashews, soaked in water for at least 4 hours

1 cup (160 g) pitted dates, soaked in water for at least 4 hours

⅓ cup (80 ml) melted coconut oil

½ teaspoon salt

CHOCOLATE GANACHE TOPPING

½ cup (120 ml) melted cacao butter

¼ cup (60 ml) coconut cream

¼ cup (20 g) raw cacao or cocoa powder

3 tablespoons (60 g) rice malt or maple syrup, or any other plant-based liquid sweetener

PEANUT "BRITTLE" (OPTIONAL)

½ cup (75 g) peanuts

1 tablespoon (20 g) rice malt or maple syrup, or any other plant-based liquid sweetener

1} Line the bottom of an 8-inch (20 cm) loose bottom or springform cake pan.

2} **To make the base:** Add the peanuts and sunflower seeds to a food processor and process until it forms small crumbs. Drain the dates and add them to the food processor with the cacao powder and salt. Process the ingredients until they are well combined. Scoop the mixture into the cake pan and press down to create a firm and even base.

3} **To make the cheesecake layer:** Drain the cashews and add them to a high-powered blender with the rest of the cheesecake ingredients. Blend on medium to high for around 3 minutes or until the mixture is very smooth and has no more chunks of nuts. Pour the cheesecake mixture on the top of the base, making sure it is level with the cake pan. Place it in the freezer for at least 2 hours.

{ CONTINUES }

EPIC PEANUT BUTTER– CHOCOLATE CAKE

{ CONTINUED }

TIP

For a simpler version, omit the peanut butter–cheesecake layer, chocolate ganache, or peanut brittle!

4} **To make the caramel layer:** Add the peanuts to the food processor and blitz for 5 seconds or until half of the peanuts are roughly chopped. Remove the blade from the food processor and set aside.

5} Drain the cashews and dates and add them to a high-powered blender with the coconut oil and salt. Blend on medium to high for around 3 minutes or until the mixture is smooth and there are no chunks of nuts or dates. Scoop the caramel into the food processor and mix with a spoon until combined. Set aside in the fridge.

6} When the peanut butter–cheesecake layer is dry to the touch and slightly firm, spread the peanut caramel layer on top. Smooth the surface with the back of a large spoon or a cake scraper. Place it in the freezer for 1 to 2 hours.

7} **To make the chocolate ganache:** Add all the ingredients to a mixing bowl. Blend with a stick blender for 1 minute or until all the ingredients are fully combined and there are no oil streaks on top. Pour onto the caramel layer.

8} **To make the peanut "brittle" (if using):** Preheat the oven to 350°F (180°C, or gas mark 4). Add the peanuts to a lined baking tray, pour the syrup on top, and use a spoon to roughly mix them. Bake in the oven for 15 minutes or until the peanuts are golden brown and aromatic. Remove from the oven and let it cool.

9} When the brittle is completely cool, break it apart into shards using your hands. Decorate the cheesecake with the brittle and enjoy! The cake can be kept in an airtight container in the fridge for 5 days or in the freezer for up to 1 month. Make sure you slice it before you freeze it as it's difficult to cut into a frozen cake!

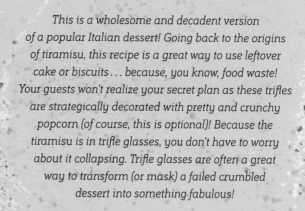

This is a wholesome and decadent version of a popular Italian dessert! Going back to the origins of tiramisu, this recipe is a great way to use leftover cake or biscuits... because, you know, food waste! Your guests won't realize your secret plan as these trifles are strategically decorated with pretty and crunchy popcorn (of course, this is optional)! Because the tiramisu is in trifle glasses, you don't have to worry about it collapsing. Trifle glasses are often a great way to transform (or mask) a failed crumbled dessert into something fabulous!

SHOWSTOPPER TIRAMISU TRIFLE WITH CARAMELIZED POPCORN

—

YIELD: 2 VERY LARGE TRIFLES
OR 4 SERVINGS

TIRAMISU TRIFLE

14 ounces (400 g) medium firm tofu

⅓ cup (80 ml) plant-based milk, such as almond, soy, or coconut

2 tablespoons (16 g) cornstarch

2–4 tablespoons (40–80 g) rice malt or maple syrup, or any other plant-based liquid sweetener to taste

2 tablespoons (28 ml) vanilla extract or vanilla bean powder

14 ounces (400 g) leftover plain cake or biscuits

½ cup (120 ml) strong black coffee

TOPPING (OPTIONAL)

1 tablespoon (9 g) coconut sugar

1 tablespoon (15 ml) plant-based liquid sweetener

1 teaspoon vegan butter

1 cup (8 g) popcorn

Cocoa or raw cacao powder, to serve

1} **To make the tofu cream:** Add the tofu, milk, cornstarch, sweetener, and vanilla to a high-powered blender. Blend until very smooth, and then pour the mixture into a medium-size saucepan. Alternatively, add the ingredients directly to the saucepan and use a stick blender to blend. Heat the mixture on medium heat while whisking for 5 to 10 minutes or until it thickens. Remove from the heat, let cool, and set it aside in the fridge to chill. If the tofu cream forms a skin while chilling in the fridge, blend it to make it smooth again.

2} **To make the topping (if using):** Preheat the oven to 210°F (100°C). Add the sugar, liquid sweetener, and vegan butter to a small saucepan over medium heat. Boil for 1 minute or until it forms a smooth caramel. Spread the popcorn on a lined baking tray, drizzle the caramel on it, and toss the popcorn to roughly coat it. Bake the popcorn in the oven for around 10 minutes and then let the popcorn cool on the baking tray.

3} **To assemble:** Arrange about ¼ of the leftover cake or biscuits to form a layer on the bottom of each trifle glass and drizzle the black coffee over it. Layer ¼ of the tofu cream in each glass. Repeat to create another 2 layers in each glass. Keep the trifles in the fridge until ready to serve.

4} Just before serving, dust the trifles with cocoa powder and arrange popcorn on top. The trifles can be kept in the fridge without decorations for up to 5 days.

BASIC CONDIMENTS

and Frostings

*These condiments and frostings
have been used several times throughout this
book because they are so versatile!*

—

*I love keeping them in the freezer to use
whenever I want to add a little more flavor
or texture to my breakfast or desserts. I often pop
the condiments in piping bags and use them to
decorate desserts for customers or loved ones!
I provide a range of frostings to suit those
who like sweet and buttery creams or for those
are prefer refined sugar-free creams.*

This Raspberry Chia Jam takes no time to make! Unlike conventional jam, this version is packed with fiber and isn't too sweet! When the chia seeds are mixed with the natural juices of the raspberries, the chia seeds form a gel that thickens the mixture and makes it a perfect jam-like consistency.

RASPBERRY CHIA JAM

YIELD: ABOUT ¾ CUP (140 G)

1 cup (140 g) frozen raspberries, defrosted

3 tablespoons (39 g) white chia seeds

1–3 tablespoons (20–60 g) rice malt or maple syrup, or any other plant-based liquid sweetener

1} Add all the ingredients to a medium-size jar or container. Mash the raspberries with the back of a fork until all juices have been released and there are no lumps.

2} Set aside for 10 minutes to thicken. Mix with a fork again to ensure ingredients are fully combined. Pop the lid on the jar or container and store it in the fridge for up to 1 week or in the freezer for up to 2 months.

WAYS TO USE CHIA JAMS
Serve it with peanut, almond, or sunflower seed butter on toast. Pipe it onto cakes or tarts as a decoration. Use it as a filling for cakes.

TIP

Substitute raspberries with other berries and fruit! Blueberries and blackberries also work well in this recipe.

Many DIY chocolate recipes use lots of coconut oil. However, when I eat chocolate, I want it to be like store-bought chocolate and not taste like flavored coconut oil! The cacao butter in this recipe takes the chocolate to the next level and adds a richness that coconut oil doesn't have. Cacao butter has a higher melting point than coconut oil, which makes this chocolate more stable at room temperature. Make sure you don't heat your cacao butter too high; otherwise, it'll be very difficult for the chocolate to emulsify.

DIY CHOCOLATE

—

YIELD: ABOUT 1 CUP (250 G)
MELTED CHOCOLATE

1 cup (225 g) roughly chopped cacao butter

½ cup (40 g) raw cacao powder or cocoa powder

¼ cup (80 g) rice malt or maple syrup, or any other plant-based liquid sweetener

1} Add all the ingredients to a small saucepan over medium heat. Heat for around 5 minutes or until half of the cacao butter is melted. Remove from the heat and let the rest of the cacao butter melt slowly by itself.

2} When the cacao butter is fully melted, thoroughly whisk all the ingredients or blend with a stick blender. The chocolate should be similar to the consistency of liquid oil and the sweetener should be fully incorporated. Set aside the chocolate to thicken at room temperature for 5 to 10 minutes or even 30 minutes if you are in a warm climate.

3} When the chocolate has slightly thickened, mix or blend it again. This is important to prevent the chocolate from blooming when it sets. Immediately pour it into molds, decorate as desired, and place it the fridge or freezer. Store the chocolate in an airtight container at room temperature (only if you are in a cool climate) for up to 1 week, in the fridge for up to 2 weeks, or in the freezer for up to 2 months.

HOW TO TROUBLESHOOT

If your liquid chocolate has separated, mix or blend it again until it is combined. If it is still separated, let it cool slightly and then mix or blend it again. If that does not work, add a little coconut cream to your chocolate and mix it until it has emulsified. The coconut cream will turn the chocolate into a ganache.

If you adjusted the amounts and your chocolate separated in the fridge, it is still good to eat! If you want to remake it, remelt the chocolate in a small saucepan over low heat. Let it cool to a lukewarm temperature, mix or blend it very well, and then set it aside in the fridge.

HOW TO CUSTOMIZE

You may substitute coconut oil for cacao butter. This will result in a strong coconut flavor, and the chocolate will melt more easily at room temperature.

If you prefer a milder chocolate, use cocoa powder. I would not recommend using any less than ⅓ cup (40 g) of powder as this amount is needed to help emulsify the cacao butter with the sweetener.

Feel free to adjust the amount of sweetener to your taste and to experiment with decorations and toppings.

CHOCOLATE GANACHE

—

YIELD: ABOUT 1¼ CUPS (430 G) GANACHE GLAZE
OR ABOUT 1 CUP (370 G) GANACHE FROSTING

Ganache is a creamy chocolate mixture made by combining cream with chocolate. The vegan version is simply chocolate combined with coconut cream. Thinner ganache can be used to glaze cakes, as a decorative drip for cakes, or to top bars. Thicker ganache can be used as a frosting and can be chilled and then rolled into truffles. Because there are different ratios and methods for each, I've listed them below.

THIN GANACHE (FOR GLAZE AND DRIPS)

1 recipe of DIY Chocolate (page 140) or 1⅓ cups (250 g) store-bought vegan chocolate

¾ cup (175 ml) coconut cream

THICK GANACHE (FOR FROSTING)

1 recipe of DIY Chocolate (page 140) or 1⅓ cups (250 g) store-bought vegan chocolate

½ cup (120 ml) coconut cream

To make the thin ganache: Add the chocolate and coconut cream to a small saucepan over medium heat. Stir occasionally to ensure the chocolate melts evenly. Reduce the heat to low if the ganache starts to bubble. Stir thoroughly or use a stick blender to fully emulsify. The mixture should be extremely smooth and there should not be any lumps of chocolate, cream, or oil streaks. Use as desired.

To make the thick ganache: Follow the method for the thin ganache and then let the mixture cool at room temperature for at least 1 hour. Use a stand mixer or an electric whisk to whip the ganache until it has increased in size and become fluffy. To thicken the frosting, add more melted chocolate. To thin it, add more coconut cream. Use as desired.

TIP

—

I used only the thick part of canned coconut cream, which makes a richer and thicker chocolate. You may use Ultra-Pasteurized (UHT) coconut cream, but this will result in a runnier ganache.

This wholesome caramel isn't too sweet as it is made with whole dates. I added coconut cream and nut/seed butters to help cut the sweetness of the dates. The liquid sweetener gives the caramel a viscosity that makes it suitable for drizzling onto desserts.

DATE CARAMEL

—

YIELD: ABOUT 1½ CUPS (350 G) CARAMEL

1 cup (160 g) pitted dates, soaked in water for at least 4 hours

½ cup (120 ml) coconut cream

2 tablespoons (40 ml) coconut nectar or any other plant-based liquid sweetener (optional)

2 tablespoons (30 g) tahini, (32 g) nut butter, or (32 g) sunflower seed butter

Generous pinch of salt

1} Drain the dates and add them to a blender with the rest of the ingredients. Blend until as smooth as possible. Adjust the flavor and consistency of the caramel as desired.

2} Use immediately or store in an airtight container in the fridge for up to 5 days or in the freezer for up to 2 months.

WAYS TO USE
Drizzle onto desserts to add decadence. Use it in your hot or cold creamy drinks to add sweetness and complexity.

This date-free caramel is perfect for those who prefer classic flavors. The coconut sugar gives it a deep complex flavor, and the butter gives it a hint of butterscotch. Without the cornstarch, the caramel is a thin drizzle consistency. Feel free to use more cornstarch if you would like a thicker caramel reminiscent of dulce de leche.

CLASSIC CARAMEL

YIELD: ABOUT 1½ CUPS (300 G) CARAMEL

1 cup (144 g) coconut sugar

¾ cup (175 ml) coconut cream

2 tablespoons (28 g) vegan butter (optional)

2 tablespoons (16 g) cornstarch (optional)

For a thin caramel: Add the sugar, cream, and butter (if using) to a small saucepan over medium heat. Stir occasionally until the sugar has dissolved. Remove from the heat.

For a thick caramel: Add all the ingredients to a small saucepan over medium heat. Stir occasionally for around 10 minutes or until the caramel has thickened. Remove from the heat. The caramel will thicken further when it cools down.

Store the caramel in an airtight container or jar in the fridge for up to 1 week or in the freezer for up to 2 months.

WAYS TO USE
The classic caramel can be used in the same ways as Date Caramel.

TIP

If you don't use vegan butter, add a generous pinch of salt.

AMERICAN-STYLE BUTTERCREAM

YIELD: ABOUT 1½ CUPS (150 G) OF BUTTERCREAM,
OR ENOUGH TO THINLY COAT AND DECORATE
A TWO-LAYERED 6-INCH (15 CM) CAKE

*This frosting is for those who prefer
a more traditional buttercream that is
rich, sweet, and buttery! Out of all the frostings,
this lasts the longest at room temperature,
making it ideal for celebratory cakes. The high
amount of sugar is needed to make the
buttercream stiff and stable at
room temperature.*

1 cup (225 g) vegan butter

2 cups (240 g) powdered sugar

1 teaspoon vanilla extract or
vanilla bean powder

Splash of plant-based milk
(optional)

1} Add the vegan butter to a stand mixer with the whisk
attachment. Alternatively, you can add the butter to a large
bowl and use an electric hand mixer. Beat on high speed for
3 to 5 minutes until the butter has increased in size and
turned pale yellow or white.

2} Add the powdered sugar and vanilla to the mixer or
bowl. Beat on low speed for 30 seconds or until the sugar
is fully incorporated. Increase the speed to high and beat
for another 5 to 10 minutes or until the buttercream is light
and fluffy. Add some milk to thin the buttercream or to add
flavor, if desired.

3} Store the buttercream in an airtight container in the fridge
for up to 1 week or in the freezer for up to 2 months.

WAYS TO USE
*This buttercream can be used to frost cakes and cupcakes. If you
thin it out with more milk, you can also use it to frost cookies, sweet
loaves, cinnamon buns, and more. Leftover buttercream can also
be baked into other cakes—just use less sugar and fat in the
original recipe!*

TIP
—

*To make the buttercream
more stable at room
temperature, use a mix of
vegan butter and softened
vegetable shortening. Whip
them together until pale
yellow or white and then
add the powdered sugar.*

CASHEW BUTTERCREAM

———

YIELD: ABOUT 2 CUPS (200 G) OF BUTTERCREAM,
OR ENOUGH TO GENEROUSLY FROST
12 CUPCAKES

I created this refined sugar-free buttercream for those who love baked cakes but don't like regular buttercream. This buttercream is stable at room temperature for around 4 hours, which I find makes it great for wedding cakes. The high amount of cacao butter in this recipe stops the buttercream from melting quickly and gives it a strong white chocolate taste.

2 cups (280 g) cashews

1 cup (235 ml) canned coconut cream

½ cup (112 g) cacao butter, melted

¼–½ cup (80–100 g) plant-based liquid sweetener, to taste

1} The night before, cover your cashews in water. Set aside in the fridge. Place the can(s) of coconut cream in the fridge.

2} Drain the cashews and add them to a high-powered blender with the cacao butter. Scoop out the thick part of the coconut cream and add it in the blender with the cacao butter and sweetener. Blend until as smooth as possible. Pour the cream into a container and add flavors or colors if desired.

3} Allow the buttercream to set in the fridge to set for at least 2 hours. When the buttercream has reached a firm but spreadable consistency, use as desired. If the buttercream is too firm, let it warm up at room temperature until it is a spreadable consistency.

WAYS TO USE
Cashew buttercream can be used in the same way as American-style Buttercream (page 146). However, it won't last as long at room temperature!

TIP

You can make this nut-free by substituting soaked sunflower seeds for the soaked cashews. To balance out the earthy flavor, add a dollop of plant-based yogurt.

Coconut cream often behaves in a similar way to dairy cream in cooking. All you need to do is chill and whip it, and then you have a super fluffy and creamy frosting! When buying coconut cream for this recipe, make sure you get canned cream that has no emulsifiers as you want the cream to separate from the water. If your cream does not whip, you may have a faulty can or the brand of cream simply does not whip.

WHIPPED COCONUT CREAM FROSTING

———

YIELD: 17 TO 18½ OUNCES (500 TO 550 ML) WHIPPED COCONUT CREAM

2 cups (475 ml) canned coconut cream

¼–½ cup (30–60 g) powdered sugar, to taste (optional)

Dash of vanilla extract

Pinch of cream of tartar (optional)

1} One or two days beforehand, put the cans in the fridge to chill.

2} Scoop out only the thick coconut cream that has floated to the top of the can. Add the cream to a stand mixer or a large bowl with the rest of the ingredients.

3} Use the whisk attachment or an electric hand whisk to whisk the cream for 5 to 10 minutes or until soft peaks form. Set aside in the fridge to set further.

WAYS TO USE
Whipped coconut cream can be served with desserts such as tarts and scones. You can also transform it into chocolate mousse if you mix melted chocolate into the cream when it's whipped. If you still have leftover cream, you can use it in quiches or curries, or dilute with water to make coconut milk and bake it into cakes.

TIP
———

Coconut cream has a subtle natural sweetness, and you may not want to sweeten it further. If you prefer to sweeten it with no refined sugar, blend coconut sugar in a blender until it forms a powder and use it in the recipe. Alternatively, add a very small amount of liquid sweetener; otherwise, the coconut cream will not whisk.

Some UHT coconut cream (with emulsifiers) whip perfectly. Make sure you chill the UHT coconut cream before whipping it.

This is an easy, versatile, dairy-free cream substitute! You only need two ingredients plus flavorings. Cashews are the best for this recipe as they are the softest nut and can be blended easily. However, you may also try using macadamia nuts.

CASHEW CREAM

YIELD: ABOUT ¾ CUP (180 ML) OF CASHEW CREAM

½ cup (70 g) cashews, soaked in for at least 2 hours

½ cup (120 ml) canned coconut cream

Flavorings as desired such as maple syrup and vanilla

1} Drain the cashews and add all the ingredients to a high-powered blender. Blend until extremely smooth.

2} If the cream is too runny for your liking, add more cashews to the mixture and blend again. If the cream is too thick, add some more coconut cream or water and mix until combined. The cream will firm up when chilled.

3} Use immediately or store in an airtight jar or container in the fridge for up to 3 days or in the freezer for up to 1 month.

WAYS TO USE

Cashew cream can be drizzled onto desserts to balance out their sweetness. For example, you can drizzle it onto breakfasts such as Peaches and Cream Sourdough French Toast (page 37). If you don't add a sweetener to the cream, you can use it in savory dishes as a cream substitute.

TIP

You can make this nut-free by substituting soaked sunflower seeds for the soaked cashews. To balance out the earthy flavor, add a dollop of plant-based yogurt.

Thank you

ACKNOWLEDGMENTS

so much!

Some people may call me crazy but creating this book has been a really rewarding and enjoyable experience! There are only a few things I love more than immersing myself in a creative project. If it wasn't for the people who have supported me over the last few decades, writing this book would've been extremely stressful. Okay, I won't lie, creating this book was very stressful at times, but I'm thankful for the support of many people.

First and foremost, to my partner Dan. Thanks for supporting me from my journey as a public servant through to sickness to a very stressed business owner. Thanks for your constant humor and for lightening up life with your absurdity! I know you don't like this emotional stuff, but I appreciate when you listened to my late-night ramblings of things I need to do, helping me on your days off work and holidays (sorry!), and helping me redistribute all those recipe tests. You know how much food waste gets to me! And, at times, I appreciate your brutal honesty and realness, ha-ha!

Thanks to my parents for fostering my passion for food and for raising me to have so many more opportunities than you could have ever imagined. I'm so grateful that you migrated from Hong Kong (China) to Australia and that we were all born in Australia! Thank you to my "in-laws" for your unwavering support for everything I do. No words can express my gratitude! Also, thanks to my two Aussie cousins, aunt and uncle, and extended Melbourne family for your ongoing support and kindness.

Thank you to my old Sydney friends who have been there for me for decades and knew me before Rainbow Nourishments. I appreciate our friendships even more now! In particular, thanks Anjuma and Jacqui! And thank you to my newer Canberra friends including Chris, Megan, Masa, Laura, Lily, Dani, and your adorable little helpers. You have made living in Canberra bearable! Thanks to all of my assistants who helped during pop-up events, weekly catering orders, and workshops. I've learnt a lot from each of you.

To my Instagram and social media friends and followers, thanks for connecting with me and for your ongoing support! It can be isolating to work for yourself, but it makes all the difference knowing that I'm connecting with genuinely kind and compassionate people. In particular, thanks to Lore, Jade, Cherie, Marisa, Bo, Sara, and Jess for the in-depth chats and your openness! I'm so grateful that Instagram connected us!

Thanks to everyone who has ever purchased a cake or treat from me, attended my workshops around Australia or internationally, and attended my pop-up dinners. You have allowed me to make Rainbow Nourishments my full-time job!

Thank you to all my social media and blog followers, particularly those who have commented or liked my social media or blog posts or sent me a little supportive message!

Thanks to the team at The Quarto Group, especially Jonathan, Anne, Renae, Jenna, and Todd. You have made this dream a reality!

Thank you to the local artisans Clay Bee Hive, Mia Sorella Textiles, and Long Lunch Linen for providing and lending me your ceramics and textiles for this book!

Also, thanks to all those people who have supported me in the past. It's been an extremely difficult journey up to this point and I am eternally grateful for your help! In particular, my late best friend Michelle—you have been my biggest support and I owe so, so much to you.

ABOUT
THE AUTHOR

ANTHEA CHENG

Anthea founded Rainbow Nourishments in 2015 to share the rainbow of ways people can nourish themselves. Under Rainbow Nourishments she has many roles, including chef, recipe developer, photographer, blogger, and food consultant. She also owned a cake business and facilitates workshops and pop-up wholefood events in Australia and internationally.

Across Anthea's social media platforms and blog she reaches people nearly 1 million times per month. Online, she shares colourful vegan recipes which are adored by vegans and non-vegans alike. Driven by her university studies and both government and non-government work in humanitarian issues, she is passionate about helping her community through light discussions about well-being and the environment.

Anthea never received any formal training in food but grew up with parents who owned restaurants and catering businesses, so food is her "first language." Almost every day in her childhood, she learned how to cook in the home kitchen and family restaurant. While she leared the basics of baking in her childhood, her expansive knowledge about vegan desserts is mostly self-taught.

Anthea is a Sydney-sider at heart but currently lives in the capital of Australia, Canberra, with her partner Dan.

INDEX